EXAM
essentials

IELTS *express*

Intermediate

Workbook

Pamela Humphreys

Richard Hallows • Martin Lisboa • Mark Unwin

THOMSON
™

Australia • Canada • Mexico • Singapore • Spain • United Kingdom • United States

IELTS Express Intermediate, Workbook
Pamela Humphreys

Publisher: *Christopher Wenger*
Director of Product Development: *Anita Raducanu*
Director of Product Marketing: *Amy Mabley*
Editorial Manager: *Sean Bermingham*
Development Editor: *Derek Mackrell*
Production Editor: *Tan Jin Hock*
International Marketing Manager: *Ian Martin*
Sr. Print Buyer: *Mary Beth Hennebury*
Project Manager: *Howard Middle/HM ELT Services*

Production Management: *Process ELT (www.process-elt.com)*
Copy Editor: *Katerina Mestheneou/Process ELT*
Compositor: *Process ELT*
Illustrator: *Bill Pandos*
Cover/Text Designer: *Studio Image & Photographic Art* (www.studio-image.com)
Printer: *G. Canale & C S.p.a*
Cover Image: *Michael Dunning/Getty Images*

Workbook ISBN: 1-4130-0959-X
Workbook with Audio CD ISBN: 1-4130-0960-3

Text Credits
Page 22: Adapted from "Two for One" by Mark Abernethy. Copyright © VIVE Magazine, 2004. Page 24: Adapted from "The Big Switch" by Christine Long. Copyright © VIVE Magazine, 2004.

Photo Credits
Page 12, left © Stock Connection, top right © Index Stock/Peter Adams, bottom right © ImageState; page 27 © Creatas/PictureQuest; page 28 © Brand X Pictures/PictureQuest; page 38 top right © AP Photo/Vincent Thian; page 54 © Stockbyte/PictureQuest; page 59 © Brand X Pictures/PictureQuest.
© Index Open: Page 14 top middle & bottom; page 20 bottom; pages 22, 24, 30, 34; page 38 top middle; page 62.
© Photos.com: Page 14 top left & right, page 38 top left; pages 43, 46, 49, 66.

Acknowledgements
The author would like to thank the Thomson team for their professionalism and support, especially to Derek Mackrell and Sean Bermingham.
Special thanks go to David Humphreys for his invaluable contribution to this book.
Thanks also go to Dr Stephen Mellor for sharing his medical knowledge as well as artistic abilities.

What's in this Workbook?

The *IELTS Express Intermediate Workbook* is intended to be used together with the *IELTS Express Intermediate Coursebook*. The units of this Workbook follow the units in the Coursebook – there are eight units, with the same topics as the Coursebook. There are also three additional units for General Training Writing – two for Task 1 letter writing, and one for Task 2 essay writing. There is also an additional unit for Academic Writing Task 1 – describing a process.

In the middle of each unit, between the Reading and Speaking sections and between the Listening and Writing sections, there is a one page Vocabulary section. This section introduces and practises vocabulary relevant to the theme of the unit. The Speaking and Writing sections of each unit contain **Language bite** boxes. These boxes contain grammar or expressions useful for that section.

The Workbook Audio CD/Tape contains recordings for the Listening and Speaking sections.

At the back of this Workbook (pages 83–104) is an answer key, including model answers for all the Writing sections, and a listening script for the recorded material.

How should this Workbook be used?

Although this book may be used in class with a teacher, it is mainly intended for students to use alone at home. The exception to this is the Speaking sections. In various places in the Speaking sections you will see a 'Study Buddy' icon, which looks like this . This icon indicates that if you have a Study Buddy, or friend that you study with, you should do this task together. If you are alone, you can still do the task, but if possible, you should record yourself using a tape recorder to listen to how well you performed.

How should you learn new vocabulary?

A large vocabulary is essential to success in the IELTS exam. To develop your vocabulary you need to record new words systematically.

The final section of each Vocabulary section, Vocabulary revision, asks you to make a note of ten new vocabulary items from the unit that you want to remember. There are a number of ways you can do this:

- Get a small notebook which you can use as a vocabulary notebook. When you come across a new vocabulary item that you need to remember, write it in the notebook. Some people like to organise their vocabulary notebook alphabetically, that is, all items beginning with A in one section, all those beginning with B in the next, and so on. A benefit of this is that when you write an item in your book, it's easy to see whether you've come across this item before. Others prefer to organise their notebook by topic, for example, words related to crime and punishment all together on one page.
- Write new vocabulary items on small pieces of paper or index cards to create flashcards, and store them in a vocabulary box.

Whichever system you use, make sure that for each item you write additional information about the word, like a translation of it into your own language, an example phrase or sentence, whether the item is a noun, a verb, an idiom, etc., the pronunciation, and any important collocations.

You should carry your notebook or flashcards with you all the time and review vocabulary whenever you have any free time – on the bus, on the train, anywhere! You can do this alone or with a friend – pick out an item and test yourself or a partner on the meaning.

Finally, one of the best ways to enlarge your English vocabulary is to read a lot outside class. Reading material is easily found on the Internet, or you could use Graded Readers. Ask your teacher for some suggestions.

1

READING

Studying Overseas

1 Introduction

Read the statements 1–6 below about studying abroad. Do you agree or disagree with them?

1 You should make sure your English is good enough before you go abroad.

2 Foreign students experience culture shock.

3 You should make friends with the people in the country where you are studying.

4 There are differences in writing in English compared to your own language.

5 You shouldn't study abroad – it's a waste of money.

6 It's a good idea to take a preparation course before you start your degree course.

2 Predicting content

A Read the first paragraph of the article below and look at the headings of the three paragraphs that follow. Which of the topics in statements 1–6 above do you think the article will be about?

B Now read the rest of the article quickly (not more than four minutes). Check if your predictions were correct.

Studying Overseas

More and more students are travelling to English-speaking countries to study. We talked to three students about their experiences and asked them what difficulties they had had and if they had any advice on how to make the most of the overseas studying experience.

Yoshiko
from Nagano, Japan

Expect some changes in approach

I found it difficult to settle into a new way of studying. I went to a university in Australia, and it was completely different from Japan. In tutorials, you are expected to be much more active – asking questions and giving your opinions – and I found it very difficult at first. The other problem was completing written assignments. Where I come from, you don't have to analyse and build arguments in the same way I needed to do in Australia – in Japan, we often work around the idea, looking at it from different angles. So it required a big change in thinking. In my opinion, it's not just your level of English that you need to work on – it's your approach to studying in general.

Get used to reading long texts

I agree with Yoshiko – the essay style was a problem for me, too. You are expected to construct your arguments in a very linear way: you need to make a point and provide support for it, then you introduce a new point. This is quite different from the style I am familiar with, but once I understood what was required of me, I was able to adapt.

Another problem for me was reading. It was very hard at first to read long texts in English. Before I came here, the longest text I'd read was only a page, but we were asked to read articles up to fifteen pages long! I was lucky – I took a course which helped prepare me for studying at English-speaking universities. We were shown techniques to improve our reading and we moved from short texts to longer and longer ones. Now I feel a lot more confident about reading in English. If you want my advice, take a preparation course before you start your main degree. You'll feel a lot more confident and better prepared if you do.

Tariq
from Cairo, Egypt

Take part in discussions right from the start

I don't have problems with reading, as I had already done a lot of that before I arrived here. What I found very hard was taking part in discussions. I could usually follow the arguments, and I knew enough about the topics, but I couldn't think of what to say quickly enough or I was too worried about making mistakes or not being understood by the tutor. Here, you are really expected to challenge ideas and give your own point of view. I have even seen students disagree with the tutor! This was all very strange and uncomfortable for me. My advice to students is make sure your English level is high enough before you go overseas, otherwise you waste a lot of time and feel frustrated because you either can't follow what's going on, or you can't take part. The other piece of advice I'd give is: don't be afraid to speak up!

Chen Fei
from Guangdong, China

3 Matching statements to options

Before the task

1 Look at the list of options in the task below – in this case, it is a list of students. Find the sections of the passage in which each option is mentioned.

2 Read the first statement and scan the sections of the passage you identified to find an idea that has the same meaning. Once you have found the idea, note the option that corresponds to that statement. Then go on to complete the rest of the task.

Task practice

Questions 1–8

*Look at the statements (**Questions 1–8**) and the list of students below.*

Match each statement with the student it applies to.

*Write the correct letter **A–C** next to each statement.*

1   found it difficult to ask questions at the beginning ...

2   found reading difficult at first ...

3   was afraid of making errors in speech ...

4   believes you need to change your style of learning ...

5   recommends additional study prior to your main study programme ...

6   thinks you can learn skills to develop your reading ability ...

7   was worried about joining in discussions even when the topics weren't unknown ...

8   thinks that you should ensure your English ability is sufficient before travelling abroad ...

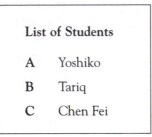

List of Students

A   Yoshiko

B   Tariq

C   Chen Fei

4 Skimming and scanning

A Look at the title of the article on the next page. What do you think a *handy hint* is?

a a small dictionary that fits in your hand

b a useful tip or piece of advice

c a custom specific to a particular culture

B Read the article quickly and see if you are right.

Handy hints for overseas students and travellers

A Studying abroad, or simply planning a nice trip to an exotic location? Unfortunately, while people might be understanding if you have problems with their language, they are less likely to be forgiving if you break the unwritten social rules. Did you know, for example, that in Japan it is considered rude to blow your nose in public (and heaven forbid you put your cotton handkerchief back in your pocket!)? You might also be studying (and socialising) with people from all over the world. A few helpful tips will ensure you avoid upsetting your hosts, or even your fellow students!

B The best advice we can give you is to learn some of the local customs of the people you will be spending time with. Let's say you have arrived in Asia and you're sharing a meal with new-found friends. You might feel very satisfied with yourself if you can use chopsticks when you're eating, but make sure you don't point with them. Many Asians consider it rude. And don't forget to check who should start the meal first: you or your hosts. Different countries have different 'rules' about this. Speaking of food, when eating in certain provinces of China, it is considered bad luck to turn over a cooked fish. And Italians like it when you show your appreciation of their cooking, so never refuse a second plateful!

C Behaviour connected with the body can be confusing because of social differences. In Muslim cultures, for example, people avoid using the left hand to give and receive. Many people in these cultures eat only with the right hand and they might consider you impolite if you use your left. But if you are given a business card in a country like Singapore, and you don't accept it with both hands, you'll be showing disrespect and a lack of interest in the person giving the card. In Britain, shaking hands is mainly done between men (and often only the first time you are introduced) but this is becoming less common these days. The Italians kiss and shake hands (but be careful, it's twice – once on each cheek), the Belgians may kiss three times, alternating from cheek to cheek, and the French? Well, whole books have been devoted to the subject!

C Scan the article to find the answers to the following questions.

1 In which country is it bad luck to turn over a cooked fish? ....

2 Which cultures avoid using the left hand to give and receive? ....

3 How many times do Belgians kiss each other on the cheek? ....

5 True/False/Not Given

Before the task

Look at the task practice questions below. For each question, skim the passage. In which paragraph (A–C) will you find the answer to each question?

1 *A*	4	7 ....
2	5	8 ....
3	6	

Task practice

Questions 1–8

Do the following statements agree with the information given in the passage? Next to questions 1–8 write

TRUE	if the statement agrees with the information
FALSE	if the statement contradicts the information
NOT GIVEN	if there is no information on this

1 People may sympathise with you about how difficult it is to study English. ....

2 People will be angrier if you don't understand their language than if you don't understand their customs. ....

3 Japanese people think it is impolite to blow your nose around other people. ....

4 It's a good idea to find out about the habits of the people where you are going to live. ....

5 It's impolite to use chopsticks with your left hand. ....

6 Italian meals usually consist of several courses. ....

7 Muslims will think you don't know how to behave appropriately if you use your left hand for eating. ....

8 In Britain, shaking hands is equally common among males and females. ....

6 Short-answer questions

Before the task

Look at questions 9–13 in the task practice below.

A Decide what kind of answer each question requires. Is it a *when, where, what, which, how many* or *who* question?

9 *what*	12 ....
10	13 ....
11	

B For each question, skim the passage. In which paragraph (A–C) will you find the answer to each question?

9 *A*	12 ....
10	13 ....
11	

Task practice

Questions 9–13

Answer the following questions. Write **NO MORE THAN THREE WORDS** *for each answer.*

9 In Japan, what should not be returned to your pocket after use? ....

10 What should you always accept when eating in Italy? ....

11 What should be taken with both hands in Singapore? ....

12 Who shakes hands most often in Britain? ....

13 How many times do Italians kiss when meeting? ....

VOCABULARY

1 Word building

A Complete the table below.

noun	verb	adjective	adverb
expectation	expect	*expected*	*expectedly*
			completely
	analyse		
		constructive	
introduction			
	appreciate		
sympathy			
	satisfy		
society			
	comfort		

B Circle the correct word in **bold** in each sentence.

1 I got a bad mark for my essay, but the professor made some very **constructive/constructively** criticisms so my next one will be better.

2 My tutor told me that it was good for a student to try and have an **analysis/analytical** approach to their studies.

3 I know that I should be more **appreciative/appreciatively** of my parents' support.

4 I tried to **sympathise/sympathetic** when my friend failed her exams, but she hadn't studied at all!

5 She left university without **completion/completing** her degree, which was a great pity.

2 Vocabulary in context

A Match the words in the box to the definitions below.

approach argument assignment bibliography challenge
degree lecture style support text topic tutorial

1 a class at university/college for a small group of students with a tutor ....

2 a piece of writing done by a student for a lecturer/tutor ....

3 a subject that you write or talk about ....

4 evidence to show that your point is a good one ....

5 a way of thinking or writing about a problem ....

6 reason given to support something ....

7 something you read ....

8 the qualification you receive after completing university level studies ....

9 to question a point of view ....

10 way of doing something ....

B Complete the sentences with the words in the box.

abstract appendix criteria draft format
prioritise project theme reduce text

1 Academic essays usually follow a strict .... of introduction, body and conclusion.

2 Extra information in a book is usually found at the back in the ....

3 If you have a heavy workload, you need to .... your tasks.

4 You look very tired, you should .... the numbers of hours you spend studying.

5 One hard disk can store millions of pages of ....

6 The main .... of the book was how difficult it is to forgive.

7 The primary school children were assigned a science .... about electricity.

8 What are the .... you are using to select candidates for the job?

9 You should always write a rough .... after you have planned your essay.

10 Academic papers usually contain a short summary at the beginning, in the ....

C Some of the words in the box above can only be used as nouns, some can only be used as verbs, and some can be used as either a noun or a verb. Write the words in the correct column. The first one has been done for you.

noun only	verb only	noun or verb
abstract	....	....
....	....	....
....	....	....
....	....	....
....	....	....

3 Vocabulary revision

Choose up to ten new words to learn from this unit and write them in your vocabulary note book. See page 3 for vocabulary learning tips.

1 Talking about likes and dislikes

A Put the verbs in the box below in order on the line. Some words may have a very similar meaning so you can put them in the same place on the line.

←————— dislike ————————————————————— like —————→

> be fond of can't stand ~~dislike~~ don't like don't mind enjoy ~~like~~
> love hate really like

Language *bite*

Expressing likes and dislikes

Verbs expressing like and dislike e.g. *like, enjoy, hate, can't stand* are followed by either a noun –

> I can't stand **housework**.
> I really like **skiing**.

or by the *-ing* form of a verb + noun –

> I can't stand **doing housework**.
> I really like **going skiing**.

When *would* is put before the verbs that express like and dislike e.g. *would like* and *would hate*, we are talking hypothetically about something we want or don't want to do and probably haven't done. *Would like* and *would hate* are followed by *to* + infinitive –

> I **would like** to travel abroad.
> I **would hate** to go skiing on my own.

Would is not used with *can't stand*.

B Look at the three example sentences below. Then use the free time activities in the box, or your own ideas to make ten sentences that are true for you.

I can't stand studying.
I love eating out.
I really hate surfing the Internet.

> eating out   going out with my friends   going shopping   going to the cinema
> listening to CDs   meeting my girlfriend/boyfriend/friends   playing tennis/football/chess, etc.
> reading the newspaper   reading novels   studying   surfing the Net   travelling abroad

1 ....
2 ....
3 ....
4 ....
5 ....

6 ....
7 ....
8 ....
9 ....
10 ....

C Organise what you want to say.
- Choose one topic from the list above.
- Think about why you like or dislike the topic and spend a few minutes thinking about what you are going to say. Make notes if you want, but don't write full sentences.
- Speak about the topic for at least thirty seconds.

2 Talking about travelling abroad

A **1.1** Listen to two people talking about travelling abroad. Does each speaker like or dislike travelling abroad?

Speaker 1 likes/dislikes travelling abroad.

Speaker 2 likes/dislikes travelling abroad.

B **1.1** Listen again. What does each speaker say he or she likes or dislikes?

Speaker 1 likes/dislikes ....

Speaker 2 likes/dislikes ....

C Now give your opinion about travelling abroad. Try to talk for at least a minute. If you can, record yourself speaking.

3 Talking about where you come from

A Complete each sentence about your home town by choosing one of the choices in bold or by adding your own answer.

1 My home town is **very small/quite big/very large/** .... and has a population of **300,000/5 million people/** ....

2 It's a **rural/industrial/** .... area so many people work as **farmers/for big companies/** ....

3 Most people live in **flats/big houses/** .... **far from/near to** the **town/city/village**.

4 I **like it/don't like it** there because **I grew up there/it's a nice place/** ....

5 I've lived there **all my life/for ten years/** ....

B **1.2** Listen to someone talking about where they come from and make notes about what they say.

....

....

....

C Talk about your home town. Time yourself and try to talk for about a minute. If you can, record yourself speaking.

> **express tip**
>
> Don't learn any speeches off by heart because the examiners will ignore anything that has obviously been memorised.

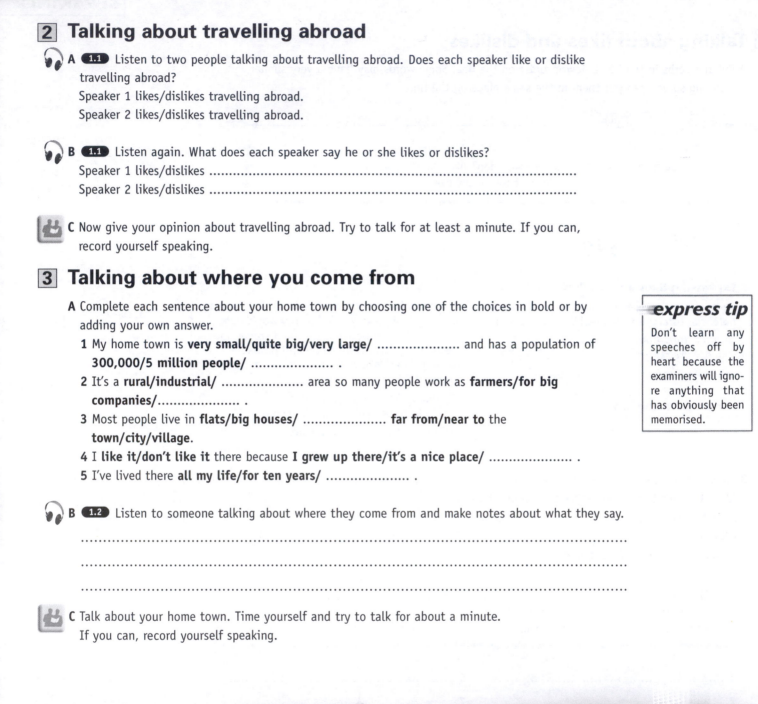

4 Talking about plans for the future

Language bite

Talking about future plans

In Part 1 of the Speaking exam, you may need to talk about your plans for the future. Look at the phrases below.

I'm going to …

I'm definitely/probably going to …

I'm planning to …

I'm hoping to …

I'm thinking about …

I might …

I (really) want to …

I'd (really) love to …

A **1.3** Listen to five people talking about their plans for the future. What does each person plan to do?

1 ....

2 ....

3 ....

4 ....

5 ....

B **1.3** Listen again and write down the phrase from the **Language bite** that each person uses to talk about their future plans.

1 ....

2 ....

3 ....

4 ....

5 ....

express tip

The examiner will be assessing you on your range of vocabulary, so it's important to use a variety of phrases in your answers.

5 Exam practice: Speaking Part 1

Before the task

Reread the information in the **Language bite** boxes in the unit to refresh your memory. Practise saying the expressions to yourself.

Task practice

1.4 Listen to five questions. Pause the recording after each question and answer aloud, using one of the phrases from the **Language bite** to talk about your personal plans.

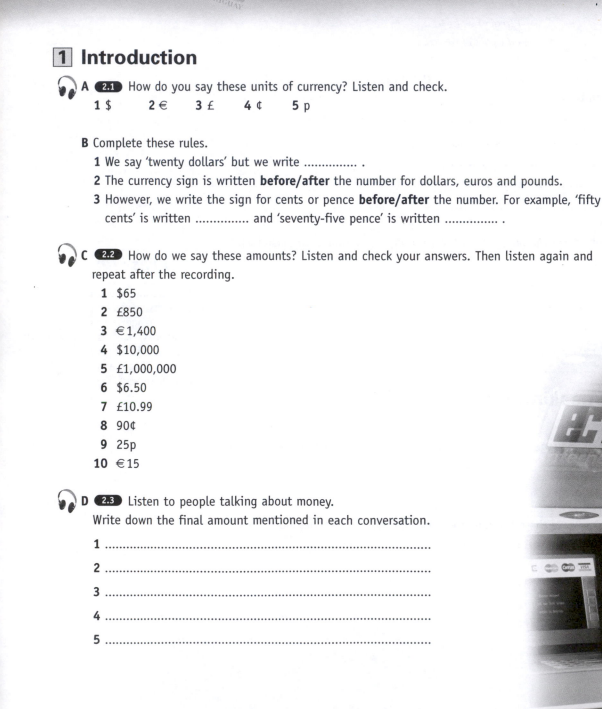

2 Shopping and the Internet

LISTENING

1 Introduction

A **2.1** How do you say these units of currency? Listen and check.

1 $ **2** €   **3** £   **4** ¢   **5** p

B Complete these rules.

1 We say 'twenty dollars' but we write ....

2 The currency sign is written **before/after** the number for dollars, euros and pounds.

3 However, we write the sign for cents or pence **before/after** the number. For example, 'fifty cents' is written .... and 'seventy-five pence' is written ....

C **2.2** How do we say these amounts? Listen and check your answers. Then listen again and repeat after the recording.

  1 $65

  2 £850

  3 €1,400

  4 $10,000

  5 £1,000,000

  6 $6.50

  7 £10.99

  8 90¢

  9 25p

10 €15

D **2.3** Listen to people talking about money.
Write down the final amount mentioned in each conversation.

1 ....

2 ....

3 ....

4 ....

5 ....

2 Predicting what you will hear

A Look at this example of a notes completion task found in the IELTS exam. Try to predict the kind of information that could go in each answer. Which ones are probably numbers? For example, number 4 looks like it is a price in pounds.

gadget name: **1** .... Scooter

purpose: to help you move faster in water

places used: underwater at the **2** .... or in the sea

top speed: **3** .... kph

price: **4 £** ....

available from: specialist shops or **5** ....

B **2.4** Listen and complete the notes above with one or two words or a number for each answer.

C A man is interested in getting an Internet connection for his computer, and is considering two kinds of connection. Look at the table describing the two types of connection for one minute and make predictions about the kind of information you will put in each answer. For example, number 4 looks like a quantity in megabytes.

QuickNet Internet Services

Service Plan Comparison					
	Price per month	Suitable for	Usage allowance	Installation cost	Modem type
heavy surfer	1 $.................	downloading 2 .... movies and online games	500MB	$200	3 ....
light surfer	$25	Using email and surfing the Web	4 .... MB	free	5 ....

D **2.5** Now listen and complete the table above with one or two words or a number for each answer.

3 Notes completion

Before the task

Look at the notes below and predict what kind of answer is required for each question. Which of them are probably numbers? Which one might be a name?

 2.6 Task practice

Questions 1–5

Listen to two men reading a catalogue and complete the notes below. Write **NO MORE THAN TWO WORDS AND/OR A NUMBER** *for each answer.*

> gadget name: **1** .... breather
>
> used by: **2** ....
>
> advantages: small and **3** ....
>
> size: 20cm – similar to a **4** ....
>
> air provided: two minutes or **5** .... breaths

4 Form completion

Before the task

A man has decided to purchase an Internet connection. Look at the application form below. Predict the type of answers that will go in each question.

 2.7 Task practice

Listen to a man buying an Internet connection and complete the form below.

Write **NO MORE THAN THREE WORDS AND/OR A NUMBER** *for each answer.*

AUSTRANET INTERNET CONNECTION APPLICATION FORM

First name: John   Surname: Mr **1** ....

Address: **2** .... Winchester Road, Sherwood, QLD **3** ....

Phone number(s): 03 924 3116 During working hours: **4** ....

Date for connection: **5** ....

Package type/name: Weekend Special   Free gift: **6** ....

Method of payment: by **7** ....

How did you hear about Austranet? From **8** ....

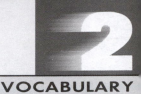

1 Word building

A Complete the table below.

verb	noun	antonym verb
sell		buy
	savings	spend
profit		lose
rise		fall
		borrow
		decrease
withdraw		

B Each of the following sentences has a mistake that students sometimes make. Rewrite the sentences correctly. The first one has been done for you.

1 The TV costed a lot of money.
The TV cost a lot of money.
....
....

2 The banks rose the interest rate again last month.
....
....

3 My father borrowed me the money to buy a car.
....
....

4 I withdrawed £300 from the bank this morning.
....
....

5 Over 50% of the price of a CD goes to the record company as savings.
....
....

2 Vocabulary in context

A Look at the following statements and decide if you would be happy (H) or sad (S) if you were in this situation.

1 You owe someone a lot of money. ....
2 You are bankrupt. ....
3 You have saved a lot of money. ....
4 You have earned a lot of money. ....
5 You father hasn't asked you to pay him back.
....

6 You can't afford to go out this weekend. ....
7 Your friend lent you some money so that you can go out. ....
8 The bank has charged you interest on your loan.
....
9 The interest rate on your loan has gone down.
....
10 You are overdrawn. ....
11 You got good value for money when you bought an item from a shop. ....
12 Your business has made a profit. ....

B Complete the paragraph with the correct form of the words from 1A and 2A.

My sister wanted to **1** .... fifty pounds from me; unfortunately, I didn't have any money and so I couldn't help. I suggested that she ask our father to **2** .... it to her, but she was too embarrassed to ask him as she already **3** .... him money from last week. She couldn't go to the bank either because her account was **4** .... by a hundred pounds. She has a good job and earns a lot of money but she always **5** .... a lot on clothes and going out. I don't think she will ever be wealthy, and if she continues like this, I wouldn't be surprised if she ended up **6** .... one day!

3 Vocabulary revision

Choose up to ten new words to learn from this unit and write them in your vocabulary note book. See page 3 for vocabulary learning tips.

WRITING

1 Using fractions and percentages

A How do you write these fractions in words? Match the fractions in numbers 1–6 with the fractions in words a–e The first one has been done for you.

1 $\frac{1}{2}$ ...e...   **a** two thirds
2 $\frac{1}{4}$ ....   **b** one and three quarters
3 $\frac{2}{5}$ ....   **c** a/one quarter
4 $\frac{2}{3}$ ....   **d** a/one third
5 $\frac{1}{3}$ ....   **e** half
6 $1\frac{3}{4}$ ....   **f** two fifths

B Write these fractions in words.

1 $\frac{1}{6}$ ....
2 $\frac{1}{10}$ ....
3 $\frac{4}{5}$ ....
4 $\frac{1}{5}$ ....
5 $\frac{2}{8}$ ....
6 $2\frac{1}{2}$ ....

Language bite

Giving approximate figures
When we are talking about numbers, sometimes we do not say the exact amount. We go up or down to the nearest whole number or 'round figure'. Sometimes we say the same idea in a different way to add variety.

51% = (just) over fifty percent/about half/ approximately half
65% = over sixty per cent/almost two thirds/(just) under two thirds
69% = almost seventy per cent/more than two thirds

C Match each amount in the box with two of the amounts

| 26%   99%   one in ten   two out of three |

1 two thirds ....
2 a tenth ....
3 almost all ....
4 10% ....
5 about 66% ....

6 just over a quarter ....
7 one in four ....
8 practically everyone ....

D Look back at the **Language bite** and write these amounts in a different way. The first one has been done for you

1 49.5%   *approximately half*
....
2 80 out of 100   ....
3 33 per cent   ....
4 one in six   ....
5 one in a hundred   ....
6 4%   ....

2 Interpreting data

A Many road accidents are caused because the driver is distracted. Look at these statistics for the top 15 reasons for distracted driving and the percentage of crashes each distraction causes and decide if the following sentences are True (T) or False (F).

Reason for distraction	Percentage of accidents caused
1 looking at crash, vehicle, roadside incident or traffic	16%
2 driver fatigue	12%
3 looking at scenery or landmarks	10%
4 passenger or child distraction	9%
5 adjusting radio or changing CD or tape	7%
6 using a cell phone	5%
7 eyes not on road	4.5%
8 not paying attention, day dreaming	4%
9 eating or drinking	4%
10 adjusting vehicle controls	4%
11 weather conditions	2%
12 unknown	2%
13 insect, animal or object entering or striking vehicle	2%
14 document, book, map, directions or newspaper	2%
15 medical or emotional impairment	2%

1 Most accidents are caused by looking at a crash, roadside incident or traffic. ....

2 Around one in ten accidents is caused by drivers looking at landmarks or scenery. ....

3 About one accident in twenty is caused because people are using their cell or mobile phone when driving. ....

4 According to the data, almost one accident in five happens because the driver is distracted by someone else in the car. ....

5 Insects or animals entering or striking the vehicle account for as many accidents as those caused by weather conditions. ....

B Complete the sentences with the correct form of *cause*.

1 Medical or emotional impairment .... 2% of accidents.

2 7% of accidents .... because drivers are adjusting the radio or changing a CD or tape.

3 Accidents .... by drivers reading maps or documents account for as many accidents as weather conditions.

4 Driver fatigue .... 12% of accidents.

5 Almost 10% of accidents .... by drivers looking at scenery or landmarks.

Language *bite*

Comparing data
Nouns with *more*, *less* and *fewer*
- For plural countable nouns, use *more* or *fewer* – *more students, fewer problems.*
- For uncountable nouns, use *more* or *less* – *more money, less information.*

Comparatives
- For adjectives with one syllable, add *–er* – *smaller, lower, higher, fewer.*
- For adjectives with two syllables that finish with *–y*, change the *–y* to *–ier* – *prettier, happier.*
- For adjectives with two or more syllables, use *more +* adjective or *less +* adjective – *more interesting, less expensive.*

Irregular adjectives
- *Good, bad* and *far* become *better, worse* and *further.*

Superlatives
- For adjectives with one syllable, use *the* and add *–est* – *the highest, the smallest, the fewest.*
- For adjectives with two syllables that finish with *–y*, use *the* and change the *–y* to *–iest* – *the prettiest, the happiest.*
- For adjectives with two or more syllables, use *most +* adjective or *least +* adjective – *the most expensive, the least convenient.*

Irregular adjectives
Good, bad, and *far* become *the best, the worst, the furthest.*

3 Making comparisons

A Complete the sentences with *more*, *less* or *fewer*.

1 .... time is needed to get an answer to an email than a letter sent by normal post.

2 In developing countries, ... people have computer access than in industrialised nations.

3 If I had a better job, I would spend .... money on computer software than I do now.

4 Fortunately, people have .... problems with Internet access now than a few years ago.

5 Even though I work hard, I have .... money to spend on clothes than when I was young.

B Circle the two words in each group that cannot be used with the word in bold. The first one has been done for you.

1 a higher/⟨less⟩/bigger/lower/⟨fewer⟩ **percentage**

3 a fewer/higher/bigger/lower **level**

3 a larger/greater/fewer/smaller/lesser **amount**

4 a higher/less/lower/fewer/greater **number**

5 a less/higher/bigger/larger/smaller/lower **proportion**

C Complete the sentences below with the comparative or superlative form of the adjectives in brackets.

1 Mobile phones are .... now than five years ago. (cheap)

2 .... percentage of Internet users in 2000 was the 18–24 age group. (high)

3 .... older people use the Internet than young people. (few)

4 .... increase in the number of goods purchased online was for books and magazines. (big)

5 Google.com and yahoo.com are two of .... Internet businesses. (successful)

4 Expressing similarities and differences

A Put the words and phrases in the box in the correct column. Two words have been done for you.

> ~~although~~ also and as ... as ~~both~~ even though have in common however not as ... as similar the same as whereas while

talking about similarities	talking about differences
both	*although*

B Look at this chart comparing computer use among children from different household incomes. Complete the following sentences with words and phrases from 4A above.

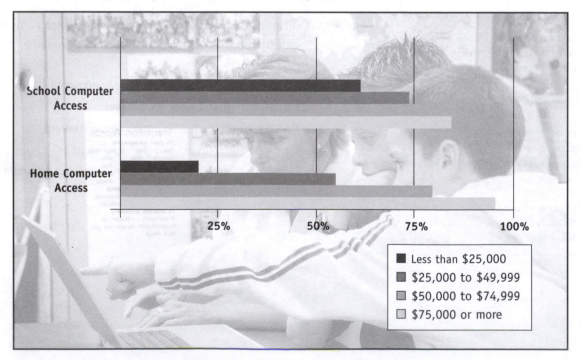

School Computer Access

Home Computer Access

25%   50%   75%   100%

- Less than $25,000
- $25,000 to $49,999
- $50,000 to $74,999
- $75,000 or more

1 Children from the $50,000 – $74,000 income bracket have very good access to computers .... at home and at school.

2 .... very few children in the lowest income bracket have computers at home, most have access at school.

3 Almost all children in the highest income bracket have computers at home, ... very few in the lowest income bracket do.

4 The two income brackets that have the most .... are the two highest.

5 Academic Writing Task 1: Describing charts

Before the task

A Look at the bar chart in the task below, and think about it for one or two minutes.

1 What information does it show?

2 What does the first column show?

3 What does the second column show?

4 What is shown on the vertical axis?

B Now look at the pie charts. What do they show?

Task practice

Writing Task 1

You should spend about 20 minutes on this task.

The graphs and charts below show the findings from a study carried out in a university about mobile phone ownership by gender and the companies used.

Summarise the information by selecting and reporting the main features, and make comparisons where relevant.

Write at least 150 words.

Total student population of university = 8,900

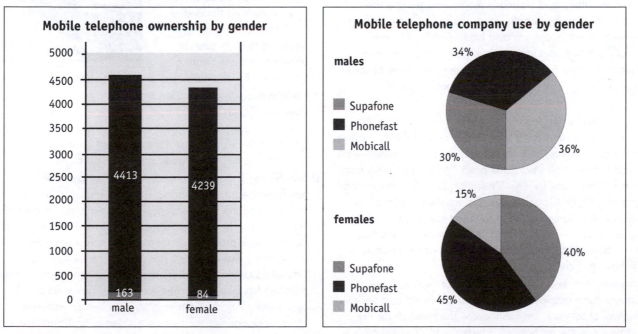

3 Jobs and Job-hunting

1 Introduction

A Look at the statements below. Are any of them true for your country?

1 Most people work full-time rather than part-time.

2 Job-sharing is common.

3 People can choose how many hours a week they want to work.

B Write four true sentences about your country by choosing one item from each of the boxes below.

men women both sexes grandparents	usually never sometimes always	work full-time work part-time bring up the children

1 ....   3 ....

2 ....   4 ....

2 Identifying paraphrasing

A Read the article about job-sharing and answer the questions on the following page, which ask you to identify paraphrased words.

Job-sharing

A Job-sharing is a concept that first appeared as a trendy idea in the fifties and basically means two people sharing one job. Previously, people either worked full-time or part-time with no other options and little flexibility to move between the two. But more recently, opportunities have begun to appear for alternatives as our lives have become more complex, expensive or stressful and as we demand more.

B The issue has arisen mainly because of the nature of the female worker. Although forty-five per cent of the Australian workforce is female, only thirty-five per cent of women work full-time, since employers have been against switching from full-time to part-time in high level jobs. In 1998, The Human Rights and Equal Opportunities Commission made a landmark decision when they found in favour of a woman who accused her employers of discrimination when they did not allow her to return to work on a part-time basis after having a child.

C Job-sharing has been seen as a cure for such economic problems as unemployment, under-employment and under-utilisation of talent in the workforce. The rewards for the employee are the promise of a better work/family balance,

the freedom to return to studies or flexibility to deal with issues related to health. It is especially popular with women nearing the end of their pregnancies, people returning to work after an absence or those nearing retirement. For the employer, the organisation still gets the full-time position covered but simply by two people rather than one. This is different from a part-time job, where the role of the position within the company has to change. The quality of the work being done does not have to suffer because it is still being done on a full-time basis.

D Job-sharing is not found in all areas of employment, but it has flourished in the financial services industry, the airline industry and the independent schooling system. Indeed, the school system has played a pioneering role with regard to flexible work practices. Since it is a female-dominated profession (almost seventy per cent of the Independent Education Union's members are women), and many women demand flexibility from their employers, many schools have successfully introduced a number of schemes, including other work policies such as carers' leave and part-time work, in addition to job-sharing.

Paragraph A

1 Which adjective suggests that something is fashionable? ....

2 Which noun means 'possibilities' or 'chances'? ....

Paragraph B

3 Which word refers to 'everyone in the country who is employed'? ....

4 Which word means 'unfair treatment'? ....

Paragraph C

5 Which two-word verb means to 'manage' or 'sort something out'? ....

6 Find a verb which means 'be affected in a negative way'. ....

7 Which noun means a period of time when an employee is not at work? ....

Paragraph D

8 Which word means something has become much more common? ....

9 Give one example job from each industry where job sharing is common. ....

10 Which word means 'general rules'? ....

3 | Matching information to sections of text

Before the task

A Read the first question below and identify any keywords. Think of any synonyms or paraphrases that could be used instead of the keywords.

B Decide whether the answer to question 1 is found in the first paragraph. Remember that it is unlikely that the question will use the exact words that are used in the passage.

C Read questions 2–6 and identify any keywords. Think of synonyms that could be used instead of the keywords.

Task practice

Questions 1–6

The reading passage on the previous page has four sections labelled **A–D**.

Which section contains the following information?

Write the correct letter **A–D** *next to each statement.*

NB *You may use any letter more than once.*

1 a list of industries in which job-sharing is common ....

2 a reference to people wanting more from their lives ....

3 a reference to job-sharing as a solution to work-related problems ....

4 reasons why some workers in particular benefit from job-sharing ....

5 a reference to one industry with a high proportion of female workers ....

6 a reason why job-sharing has become an important issue in recent years ....

> **express tip**
>
> It is possible to answer the questions correctly without knowing all of the words.

4 Reading for gist

A Read the first paragraph of the article below and answer questions 1 and 2.

1 Catharine Lumby was
  a a part-time parent working full-time.
  b a full-time parent working part-time.

2 Derek Lumby was
  a a part-time parent working full-time.
  b a full-time parent working part-time.

B Now read the rest of the article quickly without using a dictionary.

The Big Switch

For Catharine Lumby, deciding to take on the role of breadwinner in her relationship was not a difficult choice. When she discovered she was pregnant with her first child, she had just been offered a demanding new role as Director of the Media and Communications department at the University of Sydney. But she didn't see this as an obstacle, and was prepared to use childcare when the children were old enough. It came, therefore, as a surprise to Lumby and her husband Derek that, after the birth of their son, they couldn't actually bear the thought of putting him into childcare for nine hours a day. As she was the one with the secure job, the role of primary care-giver fell to Derek, who was writing scripts for television. This arrangement continued for the next four years, with Derek working from home and caring for both of their sons. He returned to full-time work earlier this year.

Whilst Lumby and her husband are by no means the only Australians making such a role reversal, research suggests that they are in the minority. In a government-funded survey in 2001, only 5.5 per cent of couples in the 30–54 year age group saw the women working either part- or full-time while the man was unemployed.

The situation is likely to change, according to the CEO of Relationships Australia, Anne Hollonds. She suggests that this is due to several reasons, including the number of highly-educated women in the workforce and changing social patterns and expectations. However, she warns that for couples involved in role-switching, there are many potential difficulties to be overcome. For men whose self-esteem is connected to their jobs and the income it provides to the family, a major change of thinking is required. It also requires women to reassess, particularly with regard to domestic or child-rearing decisions, and they may have to learn to deal with the guilt of not always being there at key times for their children. Being aware of these issues can make operating in non-traditional roles a lot easier.

express tip

With some texts, it is possible to get the gist by reading just the first paragraph. With other texts, reading the first one or two sentences of each paragraph can give you the general meaning.

5 Sentence completion

Before the task

There are two different types of sentence completion task here. For questions 1–3, you need to match two halves of sentences. For questions 4–7, you need to fill gaps in the sentences with words taken directly from the text.

Questions 1–3

Read question 1 and scan the article on the previous page to locate the section of text in which the answer will be found.

Repeat for questions 2 and 3.

Questions 4–7

Read each sentence and identify the section of text it refers to. Try to predict the type of answer you are looking for. Skim the section you have identified and look for synonyms and paraphrasing.

> **express tip**
>
> With matching or multiple-choice tasks, remove the answers you know are wrong in order to reduce the choices. This will help improve your chances of being correct.

Task practice

Questions 1–3

*Complete each sentence with the correct ending **A–F** from the box below.*

*Write the correct letter **A–F** beside each sentence.*

1 They decided that Catharine would be the primary earner because she ....

2 They decided that Derek would look after their son because they ....

3 After a period of time, Derek ....

> **A** worked part-time.
>
> **B** had to be away from home at important times in their child's life.
>
> **C** didn't want to put their child in care for long periods each day.
>
> **D** couldn't support the family financially.
>
> **E** decided to return to full-time work.
>
> **F** had a reliable job.

Questions 4–7

*Complete the sentences below with words taken from the article **The Big Switch.***

*Write **NO MORE THAN THREE WORDS** for each answer.*

4 According to studies, the number of families with the same kind of .... as the Lumbys is still quite small.

5 One reason for a change in the number of men staying home is the rise in the number of .... who are working.

6 People who have the most trouble with the change in roles are often males who link their .... with their occupation and salary.

7 Women in non-traditional roles may need to cope with the .... they might feel from being away from their children.

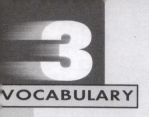

VOCABULARY

1 Word building

A Complete the table below.

verb	noun (thing)	noun (person)	adjective
train		trainer	
	employment		
			unemployed
	application		
interview			
			qualified

B Complete the sentences with the correct form of the words in the table above.

1 My son has been studying medicine for seven years and finally he's a .... doctor.

2 I sent in my .... for the position of Club Secretary as soon as I saw the advertisement in the newspaper.

3 How did your .... go? When will they tell you if you got the job?

4 John is feeling really depressed because he has been .... for almost a year and just can't find a job.

5 The insurance company told me that my .... were not suitable for the position I had applied for.

6 .... opportunities have increased because of the extra workers needed for the tourism industry.

7 There were more than fifty .... for the position of Assistant Manager.

8 All new employees are required to undertake two weeks of .... before starting work.

9 The economic recession and closure of many businesses has caused a significant increase in .... recently.

10 The bank rejected my loan application – they said my salary was too low to ....

2 Vocabulary in context

A Complete the following word puzzle by finding one word for each of the clues below. All of the words are about jobs and work. When you have finished, you will be able to see word number 12.

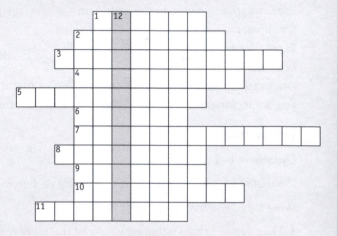

1 the money you earn regularly (e.g. each month) for working

2 this adjective means you have a job

3 this is the money an insurance company gives you if you make a successful claim

4 the opposite of part-time

5 if you have done a job before, you will have gained some knowledge, skills or ...

6 money you get from working or from investments

7 a certificate in something or the skill/ability to do something

8 you usually sign one of these before you start a job

9 in some jobs you have to wear one of these

10 if you move up in your job, it is called a ...

11 instruction or education which will help you with your job

12 something that needs to be completed before getting a job

3 Vocabulary revision

Choose up to ten new words to learn from this unit and write them in your vocabulary note book. See page 3 for vocabulary learning tips.

1 Using notes to organise your Part 2 talk

A Look at this example topic card for Speaking Part 2 and read Hilde's notes for answering the question.

> Describe an important interview that you have had.
> You should say:
>
> > what the interview was for
> >
> > how you prepared for it
> >
> > what questions you were asked
>
> and explain why the interview was important.

interview – what job? – assistant teacher
preparation – how?
– looked at notes,
– went to school website,
– made notes to take with me
what questions?
– qualifications, experience with children
– my strengths and weaknesses

#12 **B** **3.1** Listen to Hilde talk. Follow her notes and then answer the questions.
1 Did she cover all the points on the topic card? ....
2 Did she expand on them with details? ....
3 Did she speak for 1–2 minutes? ....
4 What tense did she use? Why? ....

C **3.1** Listen again and see how Hilde uses the notes as a guide. Check off each point as she talks about it. What extra details did she provide?

....

....

....

2 Talking about jobs

A Look at the sample Part 2 topic card below. Is this question about
  a your present job?
  b the job you want?
  c an imaginary job?

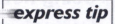

express tip

Use your notes to make sure you answer all the points on your topic card.

> **Describe a job that you think would be enjoyable.**
> **You should say:**
>   **what the job is**
>   **what tasks the job involves**
>   **what qualifications or qualities you would need to do it**
> **and explain why you think it would be enjoyable.**

B Prepare your own notes to answer the question on the topic card above. Choose a job you can talk about and make notes for each of the three points on the card.

C ●3.2● Now listen to another student answering the same question. Look at your own notes and add some ideas or make changes to improve them.

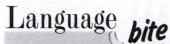
Language *bite*

Talking about imaginary situations

If can be used to talk about something possible or likely in the future, e.g.

If + present tense, ... *will/might* ...

If I get 6.5 in my IELTS exam, I'll be in England by September.

She thinks it is very possible and feels positive about it.

However, to talk about something impossible or unlikely in the future, or for imaginary situations, use *If* + past simple ... *would/might* ...

If I got 5.5, I'd need to study English in my own country for a few more months.

If I were a movie star, I'd live in a mansion in Beverley Hills. I'd travel everywhere by private jet, and I'd buy my own movie studio. It would be great!

D Now answer the questions on the topic card yourself. Try to talk for at least a minute. If you can, record yourself speaking.

3 Exam practice: Speaking Part 2

Before the task

Look at the Part 2 topic card below. Make notes to answer the questions on the card. Time yourself, and try to make your notes in one minute.

Task practice

Now answer the questions on the card yourself. Try to talk for at least a minute. If you can, record yourself speaking.

> Describe a job that you think is very important for society.
> You should say:
> > what the job is
> > what the responsibilities of this job are
> > what kind of person would do this job well
> and explain why you think it is important for society.

Follow up

Listen to the recording you made of yourself speaking, or ask your Study Buddy for comments. Check that you covered all three points and added some details.

> **express tip**
> If you don't understand the card, avoid asking *'What does ... mean?'* Ask something like, *'By ..., do you mean ...?'* or *'If I understand this correctly, it means that ...'*

4 Crime and Punishment

1 Introduction

A Match the words in the box to the definitions below.

> accused   criminal   prisoner   suspect

1 a person who is in prison ....
2 a person who has committed a crime ....
3 a person the police think has committed a crime ....
4 a person who is on trial for committing a crime ....

B Put these events in a logical order. The first one has been done for you.

a commit the crime ....*1*........
b release the prisoner ....
c convict the criminal ....
d catch the suspect ....
e defend the criminal in court ....
f charge the suspect ....

g arrest the suspect ....
h go to prison ....
i take the suspect to
the police station ....
j find the accused guilty ....

2 Identifying synonyms and paraphrasing

A **4.1** You will hear a policeman giving a talk at a local community centre about a common crime. Listen and answer the questions.
Write NO MORE THAN TWO WORDS for each answer.
1 What crime is the talk about? ....
2 When do people often find out that this crime has happened to them? ....
3 What can you do to reduce its probability? ....

B **4.1** Listen to the talk again. This time complete the extract from the talk with the exact words the policeman uses.

*... it is one of the fastest growing crimes in the world and **1** ....
You might not even **2** .... that you
3 .... of this crime until **4** .... , long
after the event has taken place. Individuals like you can **5** .... of a
successful theft if you **6** .... yourself, which is what I'm going to
talk about tonight.*

C Compare the phrases you have just written with the way the question is phrased in questions **1–3** in **A**. Note down the way in which the questions use synonyms or paraphrases rather than the exact words from the listening script, e.g. *find out* instead of *realise*.

express tip

In the exam, don't expect to hear exactly the same phrase as in the question – listen for synonyms and paraphrasing.

3 Predicting what you will hear

A Read the two multiple-choice questions in **3B** below and predict which of the topics a–d you think the police officer will talk about in the next part of his talk.

a stealing things that belong to someone by using force
b pretending to be another person
c telling lies about you to ruin your reputation
d getting access to someone's personal information

B **4.2** Listen to the second part of the police officer's talk and answer questions 1 and 2. Choose the correct letter, **A**, **B** or **C**.

1 'Identity theft' means
    A stealing a credit card and using it illegally.
    B using someone's personal details in order to make money.
    C robbing an individual rather than a company.

2 Which of these is **NOT** a reason for an increase in identity theft?
    A modern technology
    B the growth in all types of crime
    C the increase in global business

C Check your answers and think about why you rejected the other two choices.

4 Notes completion

Before the task
Look at the questions below and think about the type of information you need to listen for. Then listen to the next part of the talk and answer the questions.

4.3 Task practice

Questions 1–4

Complete the notes below. Write **NO MORE THAN TWO WORDS** *for each answer.*

Theft type	What can be stolen?
stolen wallet/purse :	**1** ...., bank cards, personal documents
burglary :	TVs, stereos, personal information and **2** ....
mail :	bank statements, credit cards, tax returns **3** ....
4 .... :	personal details

4.3 Follow up
Check your answers for questions **1–4**. Then listen to this part of the talk again and compare the words spoken with those in the questions. Use the listening script if necessary.

> **express tip**
>
> Use a process of elimination and reject any answers which aren't possible. Then choose from the one(s) that are left.

5 Short-answer questions

Before the task
Look at the questions below. Underline any keywords. Think of any synonyms or paraphrases for the keywords that you might hear on the recording. Then listen and answer *Questions 5–9*.

4.4 Task practice

Questions 5–9

Answer the questions below.

Write **NO MORE THAN THREE WORDS** *for each answer.*

5 What can you improve to reduce the risk of identity theft? ....

6 What example is given of a security feature on accounts? ....

7 What should you avoid telling people on the telephone? ....

8 Where is it safe to make Internet purchases? ....

9 If you are a victim, apart from the police, who should you tell? ....

Follow up
A Check your answers for *Questions 5–9*.

B Now look at all four parts of the listening script for the police officer's talk (page 99) and circle all the words connected to the topic of crime. Find at least twelve words and write them here.

....
....
....
....
....
....

6 Multiple-choice questions

Before the task
You will hear two students talking about a college project they are doing on fighting crime. Before you listen, look at the list of questions and options below, and try to predict the answers. Then listen and answer *Questions 1–4*.

4.5 Task practice

Questions 1–4

Choose the correct answer, A, B or C.

1 The students are discussing
   A a radio programme.
   B a television programme.
   C a newspaper article.

2 Video cameras in helicopters are used to
   A gather evidence.
   B identify suspects.
   C record crimes.

3 Who captures criminals?
   A police officers in ground vehicles
   B police officers in the helicopter
   C the recording doesn't say

4 Preliminary use of the system
   A has already started.
   B will begin shortly.
   C hasn't been decided yet.

1 Word building

A Complete the table.

noun (thing)	noun (person)	verb form(s)
burglary		burgle
		commit a burglary
kidnapping	kidnapper	
murder		murder
		commit a murder
	arsonist	commit arson
		set fire to something
vandalism		vandalise
	thief	(steal)
shoplifting .		shoplift
	robber	rob

B Answer the questions below using words from the table.
1 If you steal something using force or violence, the crime is called ....
2 Which crime in the table is sometimes committed by the owner of a failing business in order to get insurance money? ....
3 A legal synonym for this word is homicide. ....
4 If you steal from a house or office, it is called ....
5 Painting graffiti on walls is an act of ....
6 If you take a person and ask their family for money before you will give him/her back, it is ....
7 This is the noun for stealing things in general. ....
.

2 Vocabulary in context

A Questions 1–8 show eight newspaper headlines. Match each of the punishments in the box to one of the headlines.

| a caning   b community service   c electronic tagging
| d execution   e fine   f prison sentence   g stoning
| h suspended sentence

1 ... *Robber goes to jail for 15 years*

2 ... *Judge lets first time arsonist go home*

3 ... **Electric chair claims 45th victim in Texas**

4 ... **Six strokes for vandal**

5 ... *100 hours of litter collection not enough say public*

6 ... Speeding could cost you up to $100!

7 ... Latest technology informs police of criminal's location

8 ... *Village still executing adulterers by traditional punishment*

B Look at the definitions below and decide which punishments are being described.
1 The police use a small device to track the movements of the person. ....
2 You have to pay money to the government. ....
3 You have a criminal record but don't have to go to prison this time. ....
4 You are punished with death for your crime. ....
5 You are hit with a stick as a punishment. ....
6 Things are thrown at you as a punishment. ....
7 You do some work to help out in the area where you live. ....

3 Vocabulary revision

Choose up to ten new words to learn from this unit and write them in your vocabulary note book. See page 3 for vocabulary learning tips.

4 WRITING

1 Seeing two sides of an argument

A Read the following statements. For each statement, write A if you agree with it, D if you disagree and ? if you are not sure.

1 Television is a good education tool for children. ...
2 Fines are a useful punishment. ...
3 Guns should be available to everyone. ...
4 Policemen do the most important job in society. ...
5 Children who commit crimes should go to prison. ...

B Read the statements below and think about the questions that follow each one.

1 Lying is always wrong no matter whether it is a big lie or a small one.
  • What does the word 'lying' mean for you?
  • What does 'wrong' mean?
  • Is lying *always* wrong or only *sometimes*? Why?

2 There is too much violence on TV.
  • What type of violence is shown on TV?
  • What is wrong with showing violence on TV?
  • Who has the right to decide what is too much violence?

3 The police should be allowed to carry guns.
  • What problems are there if the police have guns?
  • What problems are there if the police don't have guns?
  • Is there an alternative to guns for the police?

C Here are some arguments 'for' and 'against' statement 1 above. Read each one and write 'F' if it is 'for' the statement, or 'A' if it is 'against' it.

a It is deceitful not to tell the truth. ...
b My religious beliefs tell me I shouldn't lie. ...
c You tell a lie when you don't want to embarrass yourself. ...
d Relationships are built on trust and trust comes from honesty. ...
e You may need to lie to protect industrial or state secrets. ...
f It's acceptable to lie to protect someone's feelings or be tactful. ...

D Now come up with two of your own arguments 'for' and two arguments 'against' statements 2 and 3 above.

Violence on TV	For	1	
		2	
	Against	1	
		2	
Police and Guns	For	1	
		2	
	Against	1	
		2	

2   Planning and organising your essay

A Look back at the arguments 'for' and 'against' statement 1 in 1C. In what order would you put the points to write an essay? Complete the table below.

Lying is always wrong no matter whether it is a big lie or a small one.

For	Against
1	1
2	2
3	3

express tip

Put your strongest arguments first.

B Do the same for your arguments 'for' and 'against' statements 2 and 3. Add one more argument for each side.

There is too much violence on TV.

For	Against
1	1
2	2
3	3

The police should be allowed to carry guns.

For	Against
1	1
2	2
3	3

C Look at the suggested answers in the Answer key on page 86 and compare them to your own arguments.

3   Using linking expressions

Language *bite*

Linking expressions

Linking words are like signposts – they give the reader useful information and help them find their way through the text. Linkers can signpost the following things; a contrast, a consequence, a reason or a sequence of events; they can add information, give examples and express opinions.

Here are some linking words and expressions.

because   first of all   for instance   furthermore
in my experience   therefore   whereas

A Look at the functions that linking expressions can perform. Read statements 1–7 below and decide in each case which function the linking expression is performing.

a add information   **b** show a contrast   **c** show a consequence   **d** express an opinion

e give an example   **f** give a reason   **g** list a sequence of events

1 In Britain, it is very difficult to get a gun licence, *whereas* in many places in the United States, almost anyone is able to apply for one. .....

2 Crime is increasing all over the city. *Therefore,* the police have decided to install a large number of CCTV cameras. .....

3 Capital punishment has been stopped in many countries *because of* strong opposition to it. .....

4 There are three things to do before an interview. *First of all,* research the company on the Internet. .....

5 The Prime Minister has lowered taxes considerably in the last two years. *Furthermore,* the unemployment rate continues to decline. .....

6 Prison sentences are far too lenient these days. Many murderers, *for instance,* are released in only eight to ten years. .....

7 I can't speak for everyone, but *in my experience,* this kind of situation is extremely uncommon. .....

B Look at these linking words and phrases and decide which function they perform.

> after all   because   ~~but~~   finally   for example   however   it is clear to me that
> it seems to me   next   secondly   so   then   what's more   while

Function	Linking words and expressions
add information	
show a contrast	*but*
show a consequence	
express an opinion	
give a reason	
give an example	
list a sequence of events	

4 Showing contrast

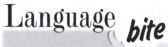

Showing contrast

These words and phrases are used to show contrast.

although   despite   even though   in spite of   however

They can be used in the following ways.

Although *violence on TV is common, people know it isn't real.*

People know violence on TV isn't real, **although** *it is common.*

Even though *some people see the death penalty as a deterrent, it isn't widely used.*

The death penalty is seen as a deterrent by some people, **even though** *it isn't widely used.*

Despite *the increased police presence in town, the crime rate is still high.*

The crime rate is still high, **despite** *the increased police presence in town.*

In spite of *the new traffic laws, people still drive too fast.*

People still drive too fast **in spite of** *the new traffic laws.*

A Complete the sentences with a word or phrase from the **Language bite** on page 36.

1 .... the large amount of violence on TV, people are able to tell the difference between real life and TV.

2 TV gives the impression that society is violent and unsafe .... the reality for most people is quite the opposite.

3 Violence is a normal occurrence nowadays on TV. .... I believe we need to be more careful about what we watch and what we allow our children to watch.

4 .... very common in popular movies, violence should not be used for entertainment purposes.

B Complete the paragraph below with suitable linking words or phrases. Then decide if the paragraph is 'for' or 'against' this statement: **The police should be allowed to carry guns.**

1 .... the police should be equipped to deal with modern criminals. The old-fashioned image of a thief wearing a black mask and carrying a bag over his shoulder is long gone (if such an image was ever true). Nowadays, many criminals are well-armed and prepared to use violence when committing a crime. **2** .... , the police must have the appropriate means to defend themselves and deal with potentially violent criminals. **3** .... , if the police are well-trained, there should be little risk. **4** .... , there are strict guidelines that the police have to follow when using a weapon and they undergo rigorous training in order to use it correctly. **5** .... , we should not encourage the police to use guns, but they should be properly equipped and trained so that they can respond appropriately when it is necessary to do so.

C Write a paragraph for the 'against' side of questions 2 and 3 in 1A on page 34 using the ideas in 2B. Make sure to use some of the linking expressions from the **Language bites**.

5 Writing a 'for and against' essay

Before the task

A Read the essay question below and underline the keywords in the question.

B Spend five minutes brainstorming arguments 'for' and 'against' the question. Decide which of these you will include in your essay.

C Decide how you will structure your essay, and in which order you will present your arguments. Make sure to include linking expressions to connect your ideas.

> **express tip**
>
> Linking expressions help guide the reader but you should not repeat the same ones too often, and they need to be used correctly or you will lose marks.

Task practice

Writing Task 2

You should spend about 40 minutes on this task.

Write about the following topic.

Lying is always wrong, no matter whether it is a big lie or a white lie.

Give reasons for your answer and inlcude any relevant examples from your own knowledge or experience.

Write at least 150 words.

Transport and Inventions

1 Introduction

A Look at the following forms of transport. Tick the ones that are commonly used in your town or city.

bicycle ... bus ... car ... ferry ... monorail ... motorbike ... scooter ... train ... tram ... trolleybus ... taxi ... underground ...*

* In British English: the underground, the tube; in American English: the Subway; in France: the Metro; in Hong Kong: the MTR (mass transit railway)

B The three cities pictured above are Bangkok, Kuala Lumpur and Singapore. Which of the forms of transport above do you think are most commonly used in each city?

2 Predicting content

A Read the introduction to the article on the next page and decide if each of the following are true (T) or false (F).
1 The text will suggest ways to solve traffic problems. .....
2 The text will mainly be about the mass transit railways in cities in Canada. .....
3 The text will be about the mass transit railways of Bangkok, Kuala Lumpur and Singapore. .....

B Underline the phrase in the introduction on the next page that tells you what the text will be about.

express tip

There will often be words in the passage that you do not know. If they are important, try guessing them from context. If they don't stop you from understanding the text, ignore them.

3 Building a map of the text

A Skim the rest of the passage. Which of the types of text map a–d below does the passage most closely follow?
a categories **b** chronological order **c** a process **d** an argument

South-East Asia on Track with Mass Transit Railways

A number of cities, including Toronto and Vancouver, are constructing mass transit railways in an attempt to overcome the inadequate road systems, where simply travelling five blocks can take over an hour. In this article, we take a look at this form of transport in three South-East Asian cities: Bangkok, Kuala Lumpur and Singapore.

A Bangkok is a thriving city with a population of six million and a further two million who travel into the city every day. Well-known for the terrible daily traffic jams, the Thai government desperately needed a transport system that would reduce pressure on the already busy roads. In 1992, city administrators embarked upon the Sky Train project, notable for several reasons.

B First of all, the government was reluctant to invest public funds in the huge project (around $1.7 billion), so private investment had to be found. In the end, a conglomerate including Siemens and the Italian-Thai Construction Company won the contract but in 1997, when the Asian economic crisis hit, the whole enterprise nearly collapsed when nervous investors wanted to pull the plug. A second major issue was the actual construction, which was taking place in the middle of the road and, whilst accidents were rare, a taxi driver was killed when a beam fell from one of the viaducts. Construction was stopped for two months and stricter safety rules were implemented. A further difficulty involved personnel who all had to be trained from scratch.

C Yet despite all these problems, the Sky Train opened ahead of schedule. Now, though, there is a further challenge for the operators: persuading the people to use the system. Compared to the buses, tickets are not particularly cheap. In order to pay the debt, the operators need to aim for a minimum of 680,000 trips a day which presents a real marketing challenge. And the Sky Train is only the first part of an ambitious plan: a further 240 kilometres of track, including an underground portion, is already in the pipeline.

D Private investment in the rail system proved to be an unsuccessful approach for Malaysia, whose government was forced to take over the finances of Kuala Lumpur's mass transit system in 2001. Although construction had already been completed, severe financial problems hit the companies responsible for the transit system. Now, the government has arranged a $5.5 billion bond to buy the assets, which will then be leased back to the companies.

E The Light Rail Transit (LRT) system has 24 stations and is a combination of tunnel and elevated track, designed to avoid impacting on existing roads. At present, around 10,000 people ride the train daily, but the target figure is 30,000. Safety and automation feature heavily: the trains are driverless, the signalling is fully automated and it is able to provide a service level of 90 seconds between trains during peak hours. In terms of safety, passengers can communicate directly with the control centre from two-way phones and every platform has emergency buttons and CCTV cameras. There is even an 'intrusion detection system' which can detect when passengers get too close to the moving trains or tracks. As well as extending the system, the government is looking at introducing an integrated ticketing system for buses and LRT as well as merging six competing bus services.

F Adding to Singapore's existing Mass Rapid Transit (MRT) is the new North East Line: a $2.6 billion, 20-kilometre underground system which was opened in 2003 by the state's Land Transport Authority. The line, including the stations, is fully automatic. It can carry 40,000 people per hour in each direction without anyone operating the trains or opening the doors at the station. Like the Malaysian system, an operating time of 90 seconds can be achieved during peak times, although currently, trains reach the stations every three minutes.

G A concept that is being explored is the use of 'multi-modal' stations. These would incorporate bus stations, MRT interchange stations, residential developments and retail space. This would allow total integration of transport systems as well as ease of transfer and should be in place by 2008. For a small country like Singapore, encouraging the community to use public transport instead of cars makes nothing but sense.

B Skim the passage again. The passage is divided into three main sections. What are these sections?

1 ....

2 ....

3 ....

C Read paragraph **A**. What is the main idea of the paragraph?

a Bangkok is a crowded city.

b Bangkok needed a solution to its traffic problems.

c The Sky Train project started in 1992.

D Read the remaining paragraphs and create a map of the text by writing the main idea of each paragraph.

B ....

C ....

D ....

E ....

F ....

G ....

4 Matching headings to paragraphs

Before the task

A Read the list of headings in the box. Look at what you decided as the main idea for paragraph A. Do any of the headings match your main idea? After choosing a heading that may be correct, read the paragraph again to see if you were right.

B Repeat the process for the rest of the paragraphs. If none of the headings seem to match the main idea in your map, read the paragraph again and compare it to the list of headings.

Task practice

The reading passage on the previous page has seven paragraphs **A–G**.

Choose the correct heading for each paragraph from the list of headings below.

Write the correct numbers i–x next to the paragraphs.

List of Headings	
i	Using technology to increase safety
ii	Training drivers from abroad
iii	Making public transport affordable
iv	Linking different forms of public transport
v	An efficient automated system
vi	Convincing the customers
vii	A series of difficulties
viii	A need for government help
ix	A badly needed solution
x	A project cancelled

1 Paragraph A   ....

2 Paragraph B   ....

3 Paragraph C   ....

4 Paragraph D   ....

5 Paragraph E   ....

6 Paragraph F   ....

7 Paragraph G   ....

5 Multiple-choice questions

Before the task

A Read question 1 and decide which city it is asking about. Using your map of the text, decide which section of the text discusses that city.

B Read the section of text you identified in 4A in more detail to find the answers to question 1. Underline the phrase(s) in the text that give(s) you the answer. You should not need a dictionary to answer the questions on the next page.

C Repeat for the remaining questions. Note that in questions 9 and 10 you need to choose **TWO** answers for each question.

Task practice

Questions 1–9

Choose the correct letter **A–D**.

1 The Thai government did not want to
  A use foreign investment for a mass transit railway.
  B rely on private investment.
  C build a mass transit railway.
  D spend public money on a mass transit railway.

2 What serious problem was there during the Sky Train's construction?
  A Workers were injured.
  B It caused significant traffic delays.
  C A motorist was killed.
  D Workers disregarded safety procedures.

3 When did the Sky Train open?
  A before the due date.
  B on the due date.
  C after the due date.
  D The passage doesn't say.

4 The biggest problem the Sky Train faces now is that
  A it isn't very popular.
  B too many people use it every day.
  C the underground section of the network still needs to be finished.
  D investors have withdrawn funds from the project.

5 When did the Malaysian government put money into the LRT project?
  A before it was built.
  B while it was being built.
  C after it was built.
  D It was paid for completely using private investment.

6 The number of passengers using the Malaysian LRT is
  A well below what was hoped for.
  B slightly below what was hoped for.
  C slightly more than was hoped for.
  D well above what was hoped for.

7 One reason the Malaysian LRT is safe is because
  A passengers can let someone know if there is a problem.
  B drivers are very well-trained in safety procedures.
  C the signalling is manually controlled.
  D it has a service level of ninety seconds between trains.

8 The opening of the first part of the Singapore MRT system
  A was before 2003.
  B was in 2003.
  C will take place in 2008.
  D has yet to be determined.

Questions 9–10

Choose **TWO** *letters* **A–E**.

9 According to the passage, Malaysia and Singapore both
  A have automated mass transit systems.
  B want a more integrated transport system in the future.
  C have trains every ninety seconds.
  D had financial difficulties with their mass transit railways.
  E have mass transit railways that go above ground only.

10 Singapore's multi-modal stations would
  A be a waste of space.
  B be close to shops and people's homes.
  C allow quick transfers from one form of transport to another.
  D only work in small countries like Singapore.
  E make no sense.

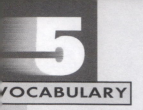
1 Word building

A Complete the table below.

verb	noun
reduce	
	communication
	intrusion
detect	
	extension
integrate	
construct	
	automation
	implementation
combine	

B Match each of the definitions below with a verb from the table. The first one has been done for you.

1 build *construct*
2 decrease ....
3 do something by machine rather than by people ....
4 enter without permission ....
5 join together ....
6 join two things to form a system ....
7 make longer ....
8 notice or observe ....
9 pass on information ....
10 start or put into action ....

C Circle the correct word in bold in each sentence.

1 To save money, the company has **implemented/ combined** cost-cutting measures in every department.

2 This machine is used to **automate/detect** dangerous levels of radiation.

3 This medicine must not be taken in **combination/ extension** with alcohol.

4 When you move to a foreign country, it can take a long time to **integrate/intrude** into the new culture.

5 Many large businesses now have **communicative/ automated** telephone answering systems.

2 Vocabulary in Context

A Complete the advert below with the correct form of the words from the table in 1A.

Security Systems Inc. – the ultimate in digital security

Imagine that people could read your business emails or listen to your phone calls. It could be happening now!
In this age of global **1** .... networks, businesses face security threats 24 hours a day. In order to prevent **2** .... from external agents, you need to be able to **3** .... any security threat immediately, and respond without delay.
With Securitech Systems' unique **4** .... of international experience and technical expertise, you will be secure in the knowledge that your business is in safe hands. Securitech Systems' technology is fully **5** .... and doesn't require human supervision, thus enabling you to **6** .... your overall security costs.
Securitech Systems Incorporated – for security solutions you can depend on.

For more information, call 555-6728, or visit www.heinle.securitechsystems.com

B Find synonyms in the advert for the words and expressions below.

1 dangers ....
2 stop from happening ....
3 outside ....
4 special skill or knowledge ....
5 safe ....
6 totally ....
7 total ....
8 expenses ....

3 Vocabulary revision

Choose up to ten new words to learn from this unit and write them in your vocabulary note book. See page 3 for vocabulary learning tips.

1 Giving your opinion

A Below are four solutions to the traffic problems in several cities around the world.
Do you think they are meant to encourage people to use public transport (PT) or to use car pooling (CP) – sharing cars? Write PT or CP for each solution.

1 In Milan and Athens, on even dates in the month (e.g. 2nd, 4th, 6th, 8th etc) you can only drive cars into the city if the last number on your car's number plate is an even number. On odd dates (1st, 3rd, 5th etc) you can only enter with cars with odd-numbered plates. .....

2 In Singapore, car owners are heavily taxed. The certificate you need to own a car can cost as much as the car itself. .....

3 In London, the council charges a tax of £5 per day to enter the inner city. .....

4 In some cities in Australia, there is an extra lane on busy roads called a 'transit lane'. You can only drive in this lane if there are three or more people in your car. .....

B Do you think these are good solutions? Rank them from 1 (= really bad idea) to 10 (= excellent idea).

1 .... 2 .... 3 .... 4 ....

Language bite

Introducing your opinion

There are two main ways you can introduce your opinion.

1 Using *that* clauses: these use *that* to introduce a complementary clause.

*I (don't) think/feel/believe **that** there are too many cars.*

*It seems (clear) to me **that** people worry too much about the environment.*

*Some/Many people believe/think/say **that** you should pay to enter the city centre.*

*In spoken English, *that* may be left out.

2 Using an adverbial at the beginning of the sentence.

***In my opinion**, public transport is too expensive.*

***Personally**, I think motorbikes should be banned.*

***In my view**, everybody should use public transport.*

C Express your opinion about the traffic solutions in A using some of the phrases in the **Language bite**. Try to talk for at least a minute and try to use different phrases for each point. If you can, record yourself speaking.

In my view, the solution used in Milan and Athens is a terrible idea. I don't really think that this would solve the traffic problem at all. It might even encourage people to buy two cars!

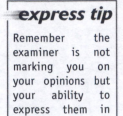

express tip

Remember the examiner is not marking you on your opinions but your ability to express them in English.

2 Agreeing and disagreeing

A **5.1** Five people are responding to the statements about travel below. Read the five statements and then listen to the recording and write the number of the speaker next to each statement.

1 Travelling by plane is the most exciting way to travel. .....
2 Mass transit railways like the London Underground are an excellent idea for cities. .....
3 In the future, people will be able to travel to the moon for a holiday. .....
4 Public transport should be free of charge. .....
5 Building more roads does not solve the problem of traffic jams. .....

Language *bite*

Adverbs for agreement and disagreement

We can make the verbs *agree* and *disagree* stronger by adding adverbs.

I absolutely/completely/fully/totally/entirely agree.

I completely/totally/really disagree.

or

I disagree completely.

I don't agree at all.

Sometimes we don't agree 100% with someone. To show you partially agree with someone you can say

I agree up to a point (but ...)

I agree to an extent (but ...)

I partly agree (but ...)

B **5.2** Listen to three extracts from the recording. Decide whether each speaker is agreeing (A), disagreeing (D) or partially agreeing (PA).

speaker 1 .... speaker 2 .... speaker 3 ....

C **5.3** Listen again to the recording from 2A. Write one phrase that was used for agreeing, one for disagreeing and one for partly agreeing. Use a maximum six words for each phrase.

1 agree ....
2 disagree ....
3 partly agree ....

D Look again at the statements 1–5 in 2A. Using expressions from the **Language bite**, say how far you agree with each statement and give your reasons. If you can, record yourself speaking.

3 Expressing levels of certainty

Language *bite*

Modal verbs

Modal verbs are *must, may, might, can, could, shall should, will* and *would*. They are followed by the base form of the verb.

> We **can travel** by train or bus in my city.

When making predictions about the future you can use *will*.

> In the future, petrol **will be** too expensive for most people to afford.

When you are not entirely sure, *may, might,* and *could* can be used to show how certain you are about an opinion.

*Raising the price of petrol **might** make people drive less often.*

*Building more roads **could** be a good solution to traffic problems, but on the other hand, those new roads **may** become just as crowded as the old ones.*

Should can be used to express your opinion by giving advice or making a recommendation.

*The government **should** charge drivers a tax for driving during rush hours.*

A Read Speaker B's response to the three questions below. Underline all the modal verbs.

1 A: Is it a good idea to offer free public transport?
   B: It could be a good idea in some cities, but it may not work everywhere.

2 A: Would it be a good idea to introduce days when some cars are allowed into the city and other days when they are not?
   B: It might reduce the number of cars, but it could just mean that people buy two cars.

3 A: Should the government keep building more roads?
   B: I don't think building more roads will help. It won't reduce the number of cars on the road. We should find an alternative to using our cars so much.

B Look again at the three questions Speaker A asks above. Using modal verbs from the **Language bite**, say how far you agree with each statement and give your reasons. If you can, record yourself speaking.

4 Exam practice: Speaking Part 3

Before the task
Read through the expressions in the **Language bite** boxes in this unit again and practise saying them.

5.4 Task practice
Listen to the seven questions on the recording. Try to speak for at least thirty seconds on each one. Give your opinion and make sure you explain the reason for it. If you can, record yourself speaking.

Follow up
Listen to the recording you made of yourself speaking, or ask your Study Buddy for comments. Check that you answered the question and explained the reasons for your opinions.

6 The Natural World

LISTENING

For further practice of Academic Writing Task 1, see page 79.

1 Introduction

A Use the words a–g to label the diagram of a volcano. Use a dictionary to help you.

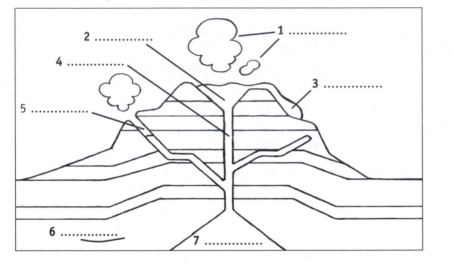

a crust
b crater
c lava flow
d main vent
e magma chamber
f secondary cone
g ash and gas clouds

B 6.1 Now listen to the definitions and check your answers.

2 Identifying speakers and attitude

A 6.2 You are going to hear some students discussing their tutorial presentations on volcanoes. Listen to the first part of the recording and describe the speakers' voices by circling the correct words below.

1 Sam is **male/female** and has a **high/low** voice.
2 Makoto is **male/female** and has a **high/low** voice.
3 Chris is **male/female** and has a **high/low** voice.

B 6.2 Listen again. Write down the expressions the speakers use to show interest, confusion and agreement.

interest ....
confusion ....
agreement ....

> **express tip**
> There will usually be a combination of men and women and high and low voices to help you in this type of exercise. Listen carefully and then match names to the voices at the beginning of the recording for this section.

3 Classification

Before the task

Read questions 1–5 on the following page and underline the keywords in each question. Then look at each keyword and think of any synonyms or ways of paraphrasing it.

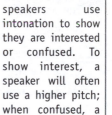 **6.3** **Task practice**

Questions 1–5

You will hear some students discussing a presentation on volcanoes.

*Write the correct letter, **A**, **B**, **C** or **D** next to questions 1–5.*

A	Sam
B	Makoto
C	Chris
D	Makoto and Chris

1 Who will be giving a presentation today? ....
2 Who researched the number of volcanoes that erupt annually? ....
3 Who talks about two volcanoes that erupt very frequently? ....
4 Who is not sure what 'subduction' means? ....
5 Who explains how the Ring of Fire was formed? ....

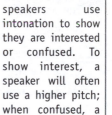 **6.3** **Follow up**

Listen to the recording again. What phrases does one of the speakers use to show surprise, and understanding? Write the phrases you hear.

surprise ....
understanding ....

4 Table completion

Before the task

Look at each answer (6–12) and predict what kind of information is missing. Is it a word or a number? E.g. question 6 is probably a number. Read the words in the notes surrounding each gap and try to think of any synonyms for keywords.

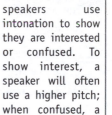 **6.4** **Task practice**

Questions 6–12

Listen to the students continuing their talk and complete the table below. Write **NO MORE THAN THREE WORDS AND/OR A NUMBER** *for each answer.*

Volcano type	Characteristics	Location
Shield Volcano	largest type – can be more than 6 .... km wide Very gentle slopes – from three to 7 .... degrees	Hawaii, Iceland, Galapagos islands
Composite Volcano	gentle lower slopes; steep upper slopes small 8 .... at top	Ring of Fire: North and South America, 9 ...., the Philippines
Cinder Cone	smallest type – less than 10 .... metres tall straight sides with 11	often found on shield and composite volcanoes as 12 ....

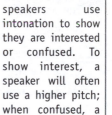 **6.4** **Follow up**

Listen again to check your answers as you read along with the listening script. Focus on the synonyms used for the words in the chart, e.g. gentle – gradual.

express tip

Take notice of how speakers use intonation to show they are interested or confused. To show interest, a speaker will often use a higher pitch; when confused, a speaker's voice usually goes down.

express tip

Remember to read the instructions carefully in completion tasks to check how many words you can write, and whether or not you can write a number.

6 LISTENING

5 Notes completion

Before the task

A The words and phrases in the box all appear in the task practice below. Match them with definitions 1–6.

> biodiversity   conservation   endangered   extinction   mammal   naturalist

1 keeping or protecting nature ....
2 a warm-blooded animal who drinks its mother's milk, such as a mouse, cow or human ....
3 a person who studies plants and animals ....
4 the complete and final death of an entire species ....
5 an adjective to describe an animal or plant at risk of dying out completely ....
6 a wide variety of animals and plants ....

B Look at the gaps in the notes below and think about what information is required for each answer. Is each answer a word, a number or a name?

 6.5 Task practice

Questions 1–6

You will hear a talk about a conservation project. Complete the notes below.

Write **NO MORE THAN TWO WORDS** *for each answer.*

<u>Details of project</u>
Name of current project: **1** The ....
Purpose of original ark: to rescue all animals from a flood
Meaning of DNA: **2** ....
Used by scientists for study and conservation initiatives
Percentage of endangered mammals: **3** ....
Naturalists protect and conserve biodiversity
Extinction leaves a gap in the **4** .... and takes a huge
amount of biological and **5** ....
DNA codes kept in a type of **6** ....

 6.5 Follow up

Read the listening script on page 102 for this dialogue as you listen again. Note any synonyms or paraphrasing used in the questions.

6 Summary completion

Before the task

Read the summary and try to understand the general meaning without worrying about the missing words. Then try to predict what word(s) can go in each gap. Read the instructions to find out exactly how many words you can use for each answer.

Remember: after you've listened and completed the task, go back and check that your spelling is correct for each answer.

🎧 **6.6** **Task practice**

Questions 7–10

You will hear how the conservation project will work.

Complete the summary below.

Write **NO MORE THAN TWO WORDS** *for each answer.*

How will it work?

Scientists plan to build up their database by taking **7** .... *from endangered creatures. If it is an animal, this will be a piece of skin. However, if it is an* **8** ...., *it will probably be the whole creature. Then, scientists will take it to be kept in the lab at very* **9** .... *Scientists are confident that the DNA will last tens of thousands of years and it is hoped that in the future, it might be possible to* **10** .... *animals.*

🎧 **6.6** **Follow up**

Listen again with the listening script on page 102 in front of you. Compare the words and phrases in the listening script to those used in the summary. Identify any paraphrasing or synonyms.

express tip

The information on the recording is always in the same order as the questions. Look ahead if you get lost. There are usually clues to help you find the right place again.

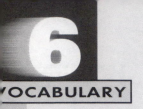

1 Word building

A Complete the table below using the words in the box.

> considerable crash decline drop faint fall fluctuate
> gentle grow level off major mild minor plummet
> plunge remarkable rise rocket shoot up significant
> sizeable slight soar stabilise

increase	
decrease	
go up and down	
stay the same	
large	
small	

B Choose the word in **bold** that best completes the sentences.

1 Since the forest on the island was cleared, the number of bird species has **soared/plummeted** from 132 to 14.

2 Because of several important scientific breakthroughs, public interest in cloning has increased **slightly/considerably** over the last several years.

3 After three years of major eruptions, there has been a steady **levelling off/fluctuation** of volcanic activity in the area.

4 Temperatures at this time of year **fluctuate/dive** between twenty-three and twenty-five degrees.

5 The stock price of the company has **shot up/crashed** to a high of $2.50 a share.

2 Vocabulary in context

Look at the graph and complete the description below. More than one word or phrase may be possible for each answer.

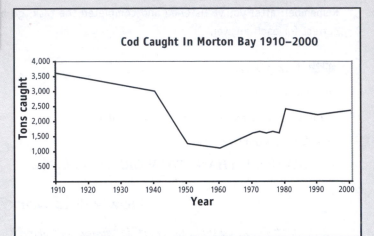

Cod Caught In Morton Bay 1910–2000

This graph shows the number of tons of cod caught in Morton Bay between 1910 and 2000. Between 1910 and 1940, the number of fish caught **1** .... **2** .... from 3,600 tons to 3,000 tons. From 1940 to 1950, the amount **3** .... to 1,200 tons, and continued to **4** .... over the next ten years to **5** .... of 1,100 tons in 1960. From 1960 to 1970, the number started to **6** .... again, and for the next ten years, **7** .... between 1,600 and 1,700 tons. Suddenly, around 1980, the number of tons caught **8** .... to a thirty-year **9** .... of 2,400 tons. Following this, there was a **10** .... **11** .... back to 2,300 tons, before starting to **12** .... again.

3 Vocabulary revision

Choose up to ten new words to learn from this unit and write them in your vocabulary note book. See page 3 for vocabulary learning tips.

1 Identifying trends

A A trend is a general pattern over time rather than just one piece of data. Look at the information below and tick ✓ the graphs and tables that show trends. Put a cross ✗ next to the ones that do not. The first one has been done for you.

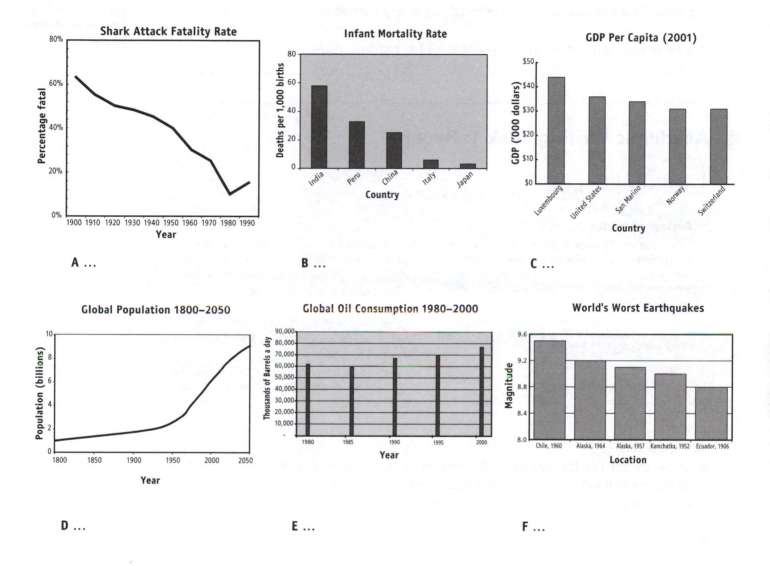

A ...

B ...

C ...

D ...

E ...

F ...

B Read sentences 1–6 below and decide if they are true (T) or false (F).

1 Graph A shows the number of people who died from shark attacks between 1900 and 1999. .....

2 Graph A shows that the percentage of fatalities from shark attacks decreased steadily for most of the last century.

3 Graph C shows the five countries that had the highest GDP in the year 2001.

4 Graph C shows that Luxembourg had the highest GDP with about 44 dollars per capita in 2001. .....

5 Graph D shows the worldwide rise in population from 1800 to 2050. .....

6 Graph D shows that the population in Europe has grown steadily during the period 1850 to 2050. .....

2 Writing introductory statements

A In Academic Writing Task 1, the first sentence is usually an introductory statement. The introductory statement gives an overview of what the graph or chart shows.

1 Which three of the sentences 1–6 above are introductory statements? ....

2 What is the first verb in all three of these introductory statements? ....

B Write an introductory statement for graphs e and f in section 1 above.

Graph e ....

Graph f ....

3 Academic Writing Task 1: Report

Language *bite*

Review of tenses

To decide which tense you need to use when describing a trend, look at the time on the horizontal axis. If the time being referred to took place entirely in the past, use the simple past tense.

> *In 1950, the population of the city **was** 2.3 million. Between 1950 and 1960 it **increased** to 2.8 million.*

To talk about a trend which started in the past, and continues until the present use the present perfect.

> *The amount of carbon dioxide the factory produces **has decreased** from 2,000 tons a year in 1990 to 1,000 tons a year today.*

Use the simple present to talk about a present fact or state.

> *The population of Australia is 20 million. The factory **produces** 1,000 tons of CO_2 a year.*

TASK A

Before the task

A Look at the chart on the next page. What information does it show? What time period does the information in the chart refer to? Which tense should you use when talking about the information in the chart? Refer to the **Language bite**.

B Decide what your introductory statement will be. Write it here.

....

Time yourself and complete the task. Try to take 20 minutes.

Task practice

You should spend about 20 minutes on this task.

The chart below shows amounts of oil consumption in different regions between 1980 and 2000.

Summarise the information by selecting and reporting the main features, and make comparisons where relevant.

Write at least 150 words.

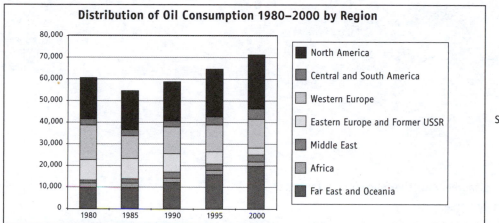

Distribution of Oil Consumption 1980–2000 by Region

- North America
- Central and South America
- Western Europe
- Eastern Europe and Former USSR
- Middle East
- Africa
- Far East and Oceania

Source: US Energy Information Agency,
International Energy Annual Report.

TASK B

Before the task

Look at the information in the table in the task below. Read sentences 1–5 and decide if they are true (T) or false (F).

1 Most of the deforestation occurred between 1980 and 1990. .....

2 The number of species of wild animals increased during this period to sixty-seven per cent. .....

3 The villagers now have more children than in 1980. .....

4 Almost everyone now has running water and electricity compared to a smaller number in 1985. .....

5 The number of villagers making a living from tourism has more than trebled since 1980. .....

> **express tip**
>
> Do not copy the sentence(s) exactly as it is on the exam paper because the examiner will not count those words in your essay. If you don't write 150 words, you will lose marks on Task Achievement.

Task practice

You should spend about 20 minutes on this task.

A small tropical island has been developed into a tourism destination.

Summarise the information by selecting and reporting the main features, and make comparisons where relevant.

Write at least 150 words.

	1980	1985	1990	1995	2000	present day
% of island covered in forest	37	24	18	18	17	17
Number of bird species	67	63	32	30	41	44
% of population (fishing)	80	78	63	42	35	30
% of population (tourism)	15	15	26	38	43	500
% houses with running water	0	35	70	95	95	95
% houses with electricity	0	0	50	94	97	97
% of school-aged children at school	34	35	32	76	80	85

7 Food and Diet

1 Introduction

To what extent do you agree or disagree with the following statements?
1 = strongly disagree, 5 = strongly agree.

1 Most children are unsure which foods are good or bad for them. .....

2 Children do not get enough exercise every day. .....

3 More young boys than girls are overweight. .....

4 Obesity in children is becoming a serious problem throughout the world. .....

5 Computers are the main reason for children not exercising enough. .....

2 Identifying the writer's opinion

A Read this quote taken from the article *Asian Children Watch TV but not their Weight*.

'*... families and schools must be involved in encouraging children to spend less time watching TV and playing computer games and more time playing games such as rope skipping, basketball or soccer ...*'

Read sentences i–iii. For each sentence, decide if it

   expresses the same opinion as the quote. (Yes)

   expresses an opposite opinion. (No)

   says something completely new, not mentioned in the original statement. (Not given)

i Team sports are better for children's health than activities like skipping. ....

ii Parents have a responsibility to make their children exercise more. ....

iii Schools should focus on education, rather than worrying about children's health. ....

B Read the first paragraph, A, of the article on the next page. Then read the following two statements.

For each statement write Yes, No, or Not given.

1 Boys aged between ten and twelve are more likely to be overweight than girls of the same age. ....

2 Girls are more active than boys. ....

> **express tip**
>
> You may find information in the text on the same topic as the question, but the opinion given is neither the same nor opposite. In this case you should choose 'Not given'.

C Read the rest of the article.

Asian Children Watch TV but not their Weight

A A new survey has found that one in four children is overweight or obese and, for boys, this figure rises to one in three. The study, conducted across four cities in Asia, investigated the health and nutrition knowledge, attitudes and behaviour of 1,815 children aged ten to twelve. The findings also showed that overweight boys tend to eat out more often, spend more time doing sedentary activities at the weekend (including using the computer and watching TV) and are more likely to skip breakfast.

B The majority of children were found to be quite knowledgeable about nutrition. In particular, when asked what their favourite foods were, the top choices were all foods which nutritionists recommend we should eat more of: rice, bread, fruit, green leafy vegetables and fish. Furthermore, many children were aware that foods containing the most sugar, fats and calories, such as sweets and fast food could be eaten occasionally, but not every day.

C What the children were far less aware of, however, was the importance of physical exercise, and many children were not doing the recommended sixty minutes or more of exercise. Researchers conclude that, whilst nutrition and health education programmes seem to be having some success in teaching children basic nutrition, the children seem to have problems utilising this knowledge to maintain a normal healthy weight. In particular, it was found that children need to understand the benefits of physical exercise and be encouraged to do at least one hour of physical activity each day.

D Georgina Cairn, of the Asian Food Information Centre, suggests that 'parental involvement and school-based programmes which fit in with the interests and lifestyles of children are key factors.' When they were asked why they didn't do more sports, children replied that homework and a lack of time were the biggest problems, as well as a preference for using leisure time for other activities.

E These comments were echoed by other academic experts. Professor Georgia Guldan of the Chinese University of Hong Kong, believes that knowledge is insufficient and stresses that families and schools must be involved in encouraging children to spend less time watching TV and playing computer games and more time playing games such as rope skipping, basketball or soccer. Dr Kallaya, from the Mahidol University in Thailand points out the mounting evidence that the worldwide rise in obesity levels is due to falling levels of physical activity. The so-called 'globesity' epidemic is causing widespread alarm amongst medical experts throughout the world. 'These patterns mirror similar trends in other parts of the world,' said Dr Molano of the Food and Nutrition Research Institute in the Philippines. The focus of nutrition materials is no longer on under-nutrition. The importance of a balanced diet and regular exercise needs to be continuously stressed. Dr Kallaya feels that life based on countless labour-saving devices such as cars and TV remote controls, combined with increased work and school pressures and a fall in the amount of physical activity leads to a predictable end-result: we are getting fatter.

F Nutrition education for young people, the researchers conclude, needs to motivate as well as inform. A key message is that fitness can be fun and can fit in with all the other activities and interests of this age group. Parental involvement is particularly crucial. Dr Poh Bee Koon of the National University of Malaysia notes that ninety per cent of the children surveyed reported that they liked to have their parents take them to their sports activities and to watch them play.

3 Yes/No/Not Given

Before the task

A Read question 1 and identify any keywords. Think about synonyms or paraphrasing for those keywords. Skim the text to locate the section of the passage related to question 1.

B Study the question and the section of text you have identified carefully. Decide whether the passage agrees with the statement in the question (Yes), disagrees (No), or doesn't express a view on the statement (Not given).

express tip

Note that in Yes/No/Not given tasks the questions follow the same order as the relevant information in the passage.

Task practice

Questions 1–10

Do the following statements agree with the views of the writer of the passage?

You should write

YES   if the statement agrees with the views of the writer

NO   if the statement contradicts the views of the writer

NOT GIVEN if it is impossible to say what the writer thinks about this

1 Most children know which foods are good or bad for them. ....

2 Children think that it is OK to eat fast food every day. ....

3 Children need less than sixty minutes exercise per day. ....

4 Health education is having an effect on weight. ....

5 Many children say they are too busy to do exercise after school. ....

6 Many doctors are worried that obesity is becoming an infectious disease. ....

7 The findings about obesity in the Philippines are similar to other countries. ....

8 Cars are the main reason children are getting fatter. ....

9 Giving people information about nutrition is not enough to change their diet. ....

10 Too many parents don't attend games when their children play sports. ....

4 Classification

Before the task

A Read the list of categories, in this case people's names, and scan the text to locate the sections of text in which these people are mentioned.

B Read question 11 and identify any keywords. Think of any synonyms for those keywords, or ways in which the statement could be paraphrased. Skim the sections of text you identified in step A to find the person who states that opinion.

Task practice

Questions 11–15

Classify the following opinions as belonging to:

*Write the correct letter **A–D** next to questions 11–15.*

A	Professor Georgia Guldan
B	Dr Poh Bee Khoon
C	Dr Kallaya
D	Dr Molano

11 The trend towards obesity is occurring worldwide, not just in Asia. ....

12 We have increasing proof that people are getting fatter because they are exercising less. ....

13 Adults in the lives of children need to persuade them to spend more time exercising. ....

14 The majority of children want their parents to accompany them when they play sports. ....

15 Increased reliance on machines and gadgets is contributing to obesity. ....

5 Summary completion

Before the task

A Read the instructions for questions 16–20 carefully to note how many words you can use for each answer.

B Quickly read the summary to understand the general meaning.

C For each answer, locate the relevant section of text and read that section again carefully. Think about the meaning and grammar of the missing word(s) and think about what word(s) from the text would fit that gap.

D For questions 21–25 read the words in the box. Note that they will usually be all the same part of speech (e.g. nouns, verbs, or adjectives), so you need to focus on the meaning of the word rather than how it fits grammatically. You need to make sure that the word not only fits in the summary, but also that it is correct in the context of the passage.

Task practice

Questions 16–20

Complete the summary below.

Choose **NO MORE THAN THREE WORDS** *from the article for each answer.*

Recent research shows that many children in Asia are overweight or obese, despite the children being aware of the importance of **16** .... and healthy eating. The survey found that the group most likely to dine away from home and live a sedentary lifestyle were **17** .... In particular, the survey discovered that although children could identify which foods they should and shouldn't eat, they were less knowledgeable about the vital role of **18** .... It appeared to the researchers that **19** .... covering diet and health were only partially successful. The researchers agreed that it is important for parents and schools to focus more carefully on the ways in which children use their **20** ....

Questions 21–25

Complete the summary below using words from the box.

To some researchers, evidence reveals that the worldwide increase in obesity is primarily a result of a decrease in physical activity. The **21** .... of the obesity problem is alarming experts who agree that it can now be considered an epidemic. It is no longer sufficient for educational materials regarding nutrition to provide information, they now need to give **22** .... as well. The message they need to provide is that exercise is also for **23** .... Essential to the success of this message is the **24** .... of parents – overwhelmingly, children report that they like their parents' **25** .... in their sporting activities.

inspiration	localisation	prevention
cooperation	education	supplement
participation	industrialisation	notification
globalisation	production	discovery
enjoyment	nutrition	

1 Word building

A Complete the table below using words from the box. Some words may go in more than one column.

show (v)	
study (v)	
research (n)	
results (n)	
people who do research (n)	

academic claim confirm confirmation consider
evidence examine expert explore facts find findings
indicate inquiry investigate investigation
investigator look into proof report research
researcher results study suggest support survey

B Cross out the words that do not collocate with the words in bold. The first one has been done for you.

1 do ~~take~~ conduct undertake + **research**

2 **provide** + evidence discovery proof confirmation support

3 **investigate/look into** + an allegation a claim an expert a problem a matter

4 provide demand need make show + **proof/evidence/confirmation**

5 show publish report inquire + **results/findings**

6 knowledge studies statistics data figures findings + **show(s)/indicate(s) that …**

2 Vocabulary in context

Use the correct form of words from 1A to complete the paragraph below. More than one answer may be possible for each gap, but don't use any word more than once.

Teaching Children to Eat more Healthily

Parents who worry about what their children eat, will be happy to hear the **1** .... of a recent **2** .... funded by the American National Institutes of Health (NIH), which **3** .... whether education programs can influence children's dietary choices. The **4** .... which were **5** .... in the journal Pediatrics were good news. **6** .... from NIH found **7** .... that education on which foods are healthy and unhealthy can affect what children eat. They **8** .... that children who attended a nutrition educational program which taught them to identify low-fat foods continued to choose heart-friendly foods three years later. The investigation **9** .... one interesting **10** .... It seems that the one food that all children in the study continued to eat, although they knew it was unhealthy, was pizza.

3 Vocabulary revision

Choose up to ten new words to learn from this unit and write them in your vocabulary note book. See page 3 for vocabulary learning tips.

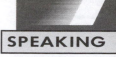

1 Structuring your talk

A Read this topic card briefly and think about how you would answer it.

> Describe a meal or dish that people in your country like to eat on a special occasion.
> You should say:
>> what it is
>>
>> how you make it
>>
>> who you eat it with
>
> and explain why you eat it on this occasion.

B Look at the mind maps two speakers made in preparation for this talk. Number the points in the mind maps in the order that you think the speakers should talk about them.

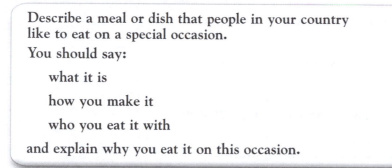

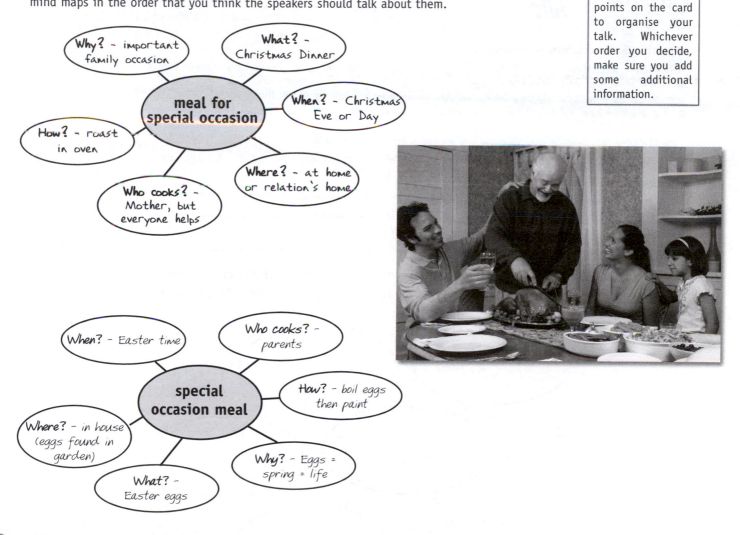

> **express tip**
>
> Although you don't have to, you might find it easier if you use the order of the points on the card to organise your talk. Whichever order you decide, make sure you add some additional information.

C 〔7.1〕 Now listen to the two speakers answering the question. Number the points in the order that the speakers mention them. Was the order the same as you proposed above?

D **7.1** Listen again and answer the following questions.

1 The speakers are talking about something that happens each time they celebrate. Which tense do they use? **a** simple past **b** simple present **c** present continuous **d** present perfect.

2 Both speakers begin with an opening sentence to give the examiner some context. What did they say?

Speaker 1 ....

Speaker 2 ....

3 Both speakers finish their talks with a short concluding sentence to wrap up. What did they say?

Speaker 1 ....

Speaker 2 ....

Language _bite_

Opening and concluding sentences

It is important to begin your talk with an opening sentence which tells the examiner straight away what you will be talking about, and provides a brief introduction to your talk. You can use the following phrases.

I'd like to tell you about ...

I'm going to talk about ...

Let me tell you about ...

The (special meal) I'd like to tell you about is ....

Concluding sentences should be used as a very brief summary of what you've said, and also as a signal to the examiner that you have finished, and you are ready for his or her Part 3 questions. This sentence will often give your own feelings towards the subject.

So I love Easter eggs because they remind me of my childhood.

So that's (the reason) why I like Christmas.

Anyway, Halloween is my favourite time of the year.

E Plan your own talk on the same topic using the mind map below. In the IELTS exam you only have one minute for this, but for this exercise you can take a few more minutes to get used to doing the task.

F Use your notes to help you answer the questions on the card. Try to talk for at least a minute. If you can, record yourself speaking. Make sure that you use mostly present simple tense, include an opening sentence to introduce the context and finish with a short conclusion.

2 Speaking Part 2

Before the task

A Look at the sample topic card below. What is it asking about? Quickly think of an experience you can talk about.

B Make notes to answer the questions on the topic card. Time yourself, and try to make your notes in one minute. Use a mind map if you find it useful.

Task practice

Now answer the questions on the topic card yourself. Try to talk for at least a minute. If you can, record yourself speaking.

> Describe your favourite place to eat out.
> You should say:
>
> > what type of place it is
> >
> > how often you go there
> >
> > who you usually go with or meet there
>
> and explain why you like going there.

Follow up

Think about these questions.

- Did you answer all the questions and add some extra information as well?
- Did you include an opening sentence?
- Did you speak for between one and two minutes?
- Did you use correct grammar and a good range of vocabulary?
- Do you think your pronunciation was clear and easy to understand?

3 Speaking Part 3

Before the task

Go back to Unit 6 in this Workbook and reread the information in the **Language bite** boxes to refresh your memory. Practise saying the expressions to yourself.

7.2 Task practice

Listen to the eight questions on the recording. Try to speak for at least thirty seconds on each one. Give your opinion and make sure you explain the reason for your opinion. If you can, record yourself speaking.

Follow up

Listen to the recording you made of yourself speaking, or ask your Study Buddy for comments. Check that you answered the question and explained the reasons for your opinions.

8 Sickness and Health

1 Introduction

A Put the words and phrases in the box into the correct groups. Two words have been done for you.

> ~~blood~~ ~~cure~~ digestive system discomfort gallbladder illness immune system
> injury intestines kidney liver lungs minerals nutrients pain recover
> stomach symptom treatment vitamins

parts of the body	health and sickness	food and diet
blood	cure	

B **8.1** Listen to the recording and check your answers. Pay special attention to the pronunciation and word stress.

2 Recognising signposts

A 🎧 **8.2** Listen to eight short extracts from a lecture. What is the speaker doing in each case? Match each extract (1–8) with the correct function (a–h).

The speaker is

a introducing a different topic ...

b about to present an example ...

c contrasting two things ...

d about to end the lecture *1*...

e adding another fact ...

f about to present a list ...

g giving an opinion ...

h talking about results ...

B Read the list of expressions below. Match each expression to one of the signpost functions listed above. The first one has been done for you.

1 although *c*

2 an example of this is ...

3 as a result ...

4 before we finish today...

5 furthermore ...

6 however ...

7 I strongly believe that ...

8 in addition ...

9 in conclusion ...

10 to wrap up ...

11 in my view ...

12 let's move on to ...

13 let's turn now to ...

14 moving on, let's look at ...

15 nevertheless ...

16 on the other hand ...

17 personally, I think that ...

18 take for instance ...

19 the result of this is ...

20 there are a number of factors that ...

21 there are several reasons for this ...

22 this means that ...

23 to finish up today ...

24 to sum up ...

25 what's more ...

26 not only that ...

express tip

Listen for signposts to help you understand where a talk is going and help you if you get lost.

3 Notes completion

Before the task

A Read the instructions on page 64 carefully to find out how many words you can write for each answer.

B Read the notes on the following page. Look at questions 1–7 and decide what kind of information is missing.

C Identify any keywords in the notes and think about any synonyms or paraphrasing you might hear on the recording.

8.3 Task practice

Questions 1–7

You will hear a talk about the liver. Complete the notes below.

Write **NO MORE THAN TWO WORDS AND/OR A NUMBER** *for each answer.*

weighs between 1 and **1** .... kg

main purpose of liver: body's **2** ....

receives **3** .... and toxins from bowels

removes unnecessary or **4** .... substances such as alcohol and some **5** ....

other roles of liver (i) stores **6** .... for emergencies

　　　　　　　　　　(ii) stores vitamins, minerals, sugars

　　　　　　　　　　(iii) helps body access **7** .... from proteins, fats, etc.

Follow up

Which expressions did the speaker use for the following functions? Listen again if you need to.

1 presenting an example　...
2 contrasting two things　...
3 introducing another fact　...

4 Labelling a diagram

Before the task

A Read the instructions to see how many words you should use to complete each gap.

B Look at the diagram and try to describe it in your own words.

C Identify any keywords on the labels and try to think of any synonyms you might hear on the recording.

express tip

Remember to keep track of the part of the diagram being described by pointing to each part as you hear it mentioned on the recording.

8.4 Task practice

Questions 8–12

You will hear a continuation of the talk about the liver. Label the diagram.

Write **NO MORE THAN THREE WORDS** *for each answer.*

gall bladder – stores bile – used to

10 ....

bile duct – gallstones sometimes

11 .... here

duodenum – start of **12** ....

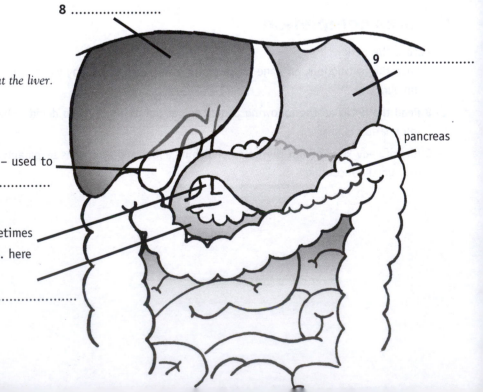

8 ....

9 ....

pancreas

Follow up

Which of the expressions in 2B did the speaker use to introduce a different topic? Listen again if you need to.

....

5 Multiple-choice questions

Before the task

A Look at the questions below. Note that question 13 is different from the other multiple-choice questions because you must choose two answers from five. Both answers must be correct for one mark.

B Identify any keywords in the questions and options and think about any synonyms or paraphrasing you might hear on the recording.

8.5 Task practice

Question 13

You will hear the last part of the talk about the liver. Choose **TWO** *letters A–E.*

13 Ancient societies believed you should take care of the liver and gallbladder to avoid
  A becoming poor.
  B becoming sick.
  C feeling angry.
  D feeling sad.
  E becoming stagnant.

Questions 14–16

Choose the correct letter, **A**, **B** or **C**.

14 Bad care of the liver can result in problems with your
  A blood count.
  B skin.
  C digestive system.

15 During weddings in some cultures the man
  A eats a piece of liver during the ceremony.
  B offers his liver to his wife.
  C promises to take care of his liver.

16 Modern medicine should pay more attention to
  A preventative healthcare.
  B liver surgery.
  C organs of the body.

Follow up

Which of the expressions in 2B did the speaker use to indicate that she was about to finish the lecture? Listen again if you need to.

....

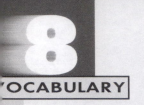

VOCABULARY

1 Word building

A Complete the table.

Verb	Noun
prevent	prevention
treat	
insure	
detect	
recover	
eradicate	
remove	
suffer	
operate	
reduce	
produce	
avoid	
cure	
medicate	
occur	
absorb	
include	

B Complete the headlines below with the correct form of words from the table.

1 **Injured actor .... well after yachting accident**

2 **World Health Organisation hopes to .... malaria by 2050**

3 **Health .... claims up 35% last year**

4 **.............. eating high-fat foods warn health experts**

5 **New water .... system introduced**

2 Vocabulary in context

Complete the article below with the correct form of the words from the table.

PharmSys announces new anti-cancer drug

Austrian pharmaceutical company, PharmSys, announced today the release of a new drug, Onctex, used for the 1 .... of several forms of cancer. Tests found that Onctex was 90% more effective than  other 2 .... manufactured by the company, provided the cancer is 3 .... early enough. In studies, it 4 .... 70% of cancers, and 5 .... reoccurrence for three years.

According to company spokesperson Andrea Firth, 'In most cases, Onctex will help patients 6 .... the need to enter hospital for a(n) 7 ...., leading to a much shorter 8 .... time. Onctex will greatly reduce the 9 .... of hundreds of thousands of people a year'.

10 .... of the drug will begin in August this year.

3 Vocabulary revision

Choose up to ten new words to learn from this unit and write them in your vocabulary note book. See page 3 for vocabulary learning tips.

1 Brainstorming arguments 'for' and 'against'

A What can't people who are vegetarian eat? What can they eat? What can't vegans eat? Write three types of food for each. Use a dictionary if necessary.

Vegetarians can't eat ....

....

Vegetarians can eat ....

....

Vegans can't eat ....

....

B Write three possible reasons why people are vegetarian and three reasons why some are not.

1 Reasons to be vegetarian

....

....

....

2 Reasons NOT to be vegetarian

....

....

....

C What's your opinion? Should people be vegetarian? Why/Why not? Complete this sentence.

I think people should/shouldn't be vegetarian because

....

2 Deciding your main ideas

A Look at this exam question and think about how you would answer it.

Some people regard eating meat as completely wrong. To what extent do you agree?

B Do you agree or disagree with the statement in the question?

List the three main areas you are going to mention in the body of the essay.

a ....

....

b ....

....

c ....

....

C Read the first paragraph of the model essay below and answer questions 1–3.

> *Vegetarian diets have become very popular as a lifestyle choice in recent years. I personally believe there are several arguments in favour of vegetarianism: health issues, the ethical/religious argument and environmental factors.*

1 Does the essay agree or disagree with the statement?

....

2 List the three main areas this student is going to mention in the body of the essay.

a ....

b ....

c ....

3 Compare these ideas with your own ideas in B above. Were any the same as your ideas?

D Use your notes from 2B to write an opening paragraph for the essay question.

....

....

....

....

....

....

....

....

....

....

....

....

E Now read the last paragraph of the model essay. Does the writer mention the same ideas in the conclusion as s/he did in the introduction?

In conclusion, modern ideas about health, environmental concerns and the ethical treatment of animals have persuaded an increasing number of people in recent years to turn away from a meat-based diet. I myself am vegetarian and believe the benefits far outweigh the restrictions.

3 Structuring an agree or disagree essay

A Read the whole essay below. Match the five different parts of an essay (1-5) to the five paragraphs a–e below.

1 a short summary and restatement of the argument …

2 supporting argument (environmental reasons) …

3 a clear statement of your view, and a rewriting of the original question in your own words …

4 supporting argument (ethical/religious reasons) …

5 supporting argument (health reasons) …

express tip

The ideas listed in the opening of your essay should be covered in the main body of the essay. Your opening and conclusion should contain the same main points.

a *Vegetarian diets have become very popular as a lifestyle choice in recent years. I personally believe there are several arguments in favour of vegetarianism: health issues, the ethical/religious argument and environmental factors.*

b *One of the most controversial issues of recent years has been the increase in the number of health scares related to the food industry. One example in the UK was Mad Cow Disease and there are many others which we are less aware of. These are obvious reasons to avoid meat. Furthermore, the health benefits of vegetarianism include lower risks of heart disease and cancers such as colon cancer. The risk of obesity and high blood pressure is also reduced.*

c *In addition to the health issues, many people choose vegetarianism because they feel that we should treat animals in a humane way. A number of religions, including Buddhism and Judaism, have teachings on the humane treatment of animals or strict rules about diet. Some people say that animals have rights and we shouldn't make them suffer. Chickens, for instance, are often kept in crowded rooms of tiny cages (called 'battery farms'), which leads to ill-health, short life-span and distress.*

d *Another reason for the increase in vegetarianism is a greater awareness of our impact on the environment. A well-documented problem is the global destruction of forests to provide pasture for meat production. Also, it is argued that raising animals for food is an inefficient way to feed the world population. For example, research shows that one acre of pasture produces approximately 165 pounds of beef, compared to 20,000 pounds of potatoes.*

e *In conclusion, modern ideas about heath, environmental concerns and the ethical treatment of animals have persuaded an increasing number of people in recent years to turn away from a meat-based diet. I myself am vegetarian and believe the benefits far outweigh the restrictions.*

Language *bite*

Linking expressions

In Task 2 of the Academic Writing exam, you need to support the opinion you express by providing examples. You can use these phrases:

to introduce an example
*for example   for instance   including
for one thing   another example of this is*

to introduce an additional point
also   furthermore   in addition to this   moreover

to describe a cause
(another) reason (for this) is   because (of/due to)

to describe a result
*the result of this is   this leads to   consequently
as a result   this means that*

B Read the essay again.

1 Circle the words and phrases in the essay which are used to introduce examples.

2 Underline the words and phrases which are used to introduce an opinion.

C Complete the summary by choosing the correct word or phrase in **bold**.

> *Vegetarians often argue that people should not eat meat. They feel that eating meat is wrong.* **1 However/Consequently** *I personally believe that a meat-based diet is a matter of choice. In modern life, people can choose to eat whatever they like,* **2 including/in addition to** *meat. In fact, eating is one of the great pleasures of life.* **3 For instance/Consequently**, *we can enjoy cuisine from all around the world. Why, therefore, should we restrict ourselves to one kind of diet? Some people say that vegetarianism is the healthiest way to live.* **4 However/Moreover** *humans are not herbivorous nor are they strictly carnivorous. Humans are omnivorous: we are designed to eat a variety of things.* **5 One example/For one thing** *which supports this view is our dental system. We are equipped with both grinding teeth and sharp teeth to grind plant products and bite meat.* **6 Another reason for/This means that** *eating meat is for its high protein content which is difficult to get without consuming meat.*

express tip

Many of the expressions you can use to introduce your ideas in the IELTS Speaking exam can also be used to introduce your ideas in the essay. See the list in the **Language bite** on page 68 for examples.

4 Writing Task 2: 'Agree or disagree' essay

Before the task

A Read the question below and decide whether you agree or disagree with the statement. Make a list of reasons to support your position, and decide on examples to back up each reason.

B Plan your essay based on the suggested five-part structure for an 'agree or disagree' question described in 3A above. Choose your three strongest arguments to include and decide which order you will write about them. Plan what you will say in your introduction and conclusion.

Task practice

You should spend about 40 minutes on this task.

Write about the following topic.

Testing on animals is common practice for products such as cosmetics or drugs. Some people regard testing on animals as completely wrong and inhumane and they believe it should not be allowed.

Do you agree or disagree with this statement?

Give reasons for your answer and inlcude any relevant examples from your own knowledge or experience.

Write at least 150 words.

express tip

Remember to start your conclusion using expressions like *in conclusion* and *in summary*.

Writing a Letter of Request

1A

1 Understanding the question

A Questions a–d are four examples of General Training Task 1 questions. For questions b–d, complete the table below by identifying the sender, the receiver, the level of formality required: formal (F), semi-formal (SF) or informal (I), and the type of request: a favour, permission or information.

	sender	receiver	level of formality	type of request
a	*student*	*school administration*	*F*	*information*
b				
c				
d				

a *You are planning to go and study English at a school overseas. You would like some information about their courses.*
Write a letter to the school. In your letter
  - *ask about the school*
  - *say what kind of accommodation you want*
  - *mention any special requests you have (for example diet).*

b *You are taking a course at a local college. The deadline for your project was last week but you haven't finished it.*
Write a letter to your lecturer. In your letter
  - *introduce yourself*
  - *explain why you haven't handed in the project yet*
  - *request more time to do it.*

c *You are renting a flat from an agency. Your contract was for one year but you need to leave the flat four months early.*
Write a letter to the agency. In your letter
  - *introduce yourself*
  - *ask to leave the flat before the contract finishes*
  - *explain why you need to break the contract.*

d *Your parents are arriving to visit you next week but you are working at the time they arrive.*
Write a letter to a friend. In your letter
  - *explain the situation*
  - *ask him/her to meet your parents at the airport*
  - *offer to help your friend in the future.*

> **express tip**
>
> IELTS General Training Task 1 questions are divided into two parts: the situation, which gives you information to explain the context, and the task, which tells you what you need to include in your letter.

B Look again at questions b–d in exercise 1A. Circle the key words in the situation. Underline the verbs that tell you what to do. Here is an example for question a:

You are *planning to go* and *study English* at a school *overseas*. You would like some *information* about their *courses*.

Write a letter to the school. In your letter
- **ask** about the course and the teachers
- **explain** what kind of accommodation you want
- **mention** any special requests you may have.

2 Using appropriate language and organisation

Language *bite*

Polite expressions for letter writing

There are many standard phrases used in polite letters.

making requests
Would you mind ... ing?
Would it be possible to ...?
I would be extremely grateful if you could ...
I was wondering if you could ...

apologising and asking for understanding
I'm afraid that ...
Unfortunately, ...
I hope you can understand (my situation).
I'm sorry for any inconvenience caused.

showing understanding
I understand/realise that ...
I'm aware that ...

introducing information
As you know, ...
As I'm sure you are aware, ...

closing
Yours sincerely/Yours faithfully
I look forward to hearing from you soon.

A Here is an example letter for situation c in 1A. Complete the letter with appropriate phrases from the **Language bite**.

Dear Sir or Madam,

My name is Hiroshi Kobayashi and I have been renting the flat in Tree Avenue from you for the past seven months. **1** .... I have been a good tenant during this period. I always pay my rent on time and look after the flat.

My rental agreement with you was for one year and the contract ends in February. **2** ...., I have just heard that I will need to leave the flat in October, which is, in fact, four months early. The reason for this is that my boss has asked me to go back to Japan earlier than planned and I am afraid this is beyond my control.

As I am now unable to stay here until the end of the contract, **3** .... release me from it early. **4** .... this is not normally allowed but **5** .... and still return my deposit.

6 ....

Hiroshi Kobayashi

B Look again at the sample answer on the previous page and complete the checklist below.

Did the writer

1 write more than 150 words?

2 complete the task in the question?

3 use three main paragraphs – 1. introduction and reason; 2. explanation of situation or problem; 3. action required?

4 use the correct level of formality?

express tip

Remember that you don't need to write your address at the top of the letter. Just begin with the greeting: *Dear ... ,*

C The following letter responds to situation b in 1A. Rewrite it to make it more formal.

Hi Ms McCall,

How are you? It's me, Cao Ying here. Do you remember me? I'm the talkative student in your E3K biology class at Shafton College. I need to ask you a favour because I haven't done my assignment yet. We were supposed to hand it in tomorrow but I've been so busy and I had so many other things to do that I haven't even started it yet!!! Anyway, the reason I'm writing is to ask for a bit more time. Can I hand it in next week instead? Please?

Best wishes

Cao Ying

3 Writing a letter of request

Before the task

A Read the question below and identify the situation and the task. Underline the keywords in the task.

B Spend five minutes brainstorming details to include in your response. Decide which of these you will include in your letter.

C Decide how you will structure your letter and what you will include in each paragraph. Make sure you include the polite phrases covered in this unit.

Task practice

You should spend about 20 minutes on this task.

> **You are planning to go and study English at a school overseas. You would like some information about their courses.**
>
> **Write a letter to the school. In your letter**
> * **ask about the school**
> * **say what kind of accommodation you want**
> * **mention any special requests you have (for example diet).**

Write at least 150 words.

You do **NOT** need to write any addresses.

Begin your letter as follows:

Dear ...

Follow up

Read through your letter to check spelling and grammar. Make sure you have written at least 150 words.

Writing a Letter of Complaint

1 Introducing a complaint

A Look at the sample General Training Writing Task 1 below.

1 Who is the writer?
2 Who is the receiver?
3 What level of formality should be used – formal, semi-formal, or informal?

The air-conditioner in your flat broke three weeks ago and it is the middle of summer. You asked the landlord to repair it and he promised to send someone but no-one has contacted you yet.

Write a letter to the landlord complaining about the situation. In your letter
- *explain the problem*
- *remind the landlord about his promise*
- *say what you want him to do.*

B Read the first sentence of a letter based on the task above and underline the expression the writer uses to introduce the complaint.

Dear Mr Jones,

I am writing to complain about our air-conditioning, which has now been broken for over three weeks.

C Write the first sentence of a letter responding to the following first part of a Task 1 question.

You are renting a fully-furnished flat and your TV broke a week ago. You have phoned the landlady many times and left several messages about the problem but she never contacts you.

2 Describing your complaint

Language *bite*

Using infinitives in letters of complaint

The infinitive – *to* + verb, is a common structure in letters of complaint. It is used in several ways:

to talk about what someone has said or agreed upon
You promised to send someone to fix it. You agreed to call me the next day.

to ask someone to do something
I'd like you to call me. I want you to fix it. Please tell him to do it right away.

to express purpose
I'm writing to complain about ...;
I called you to discuss this, but you didn't answer the phone.

A Use the prompts below to write sentences. In many cases you will use the infinitive, in others you may need to change the tense of the verb, or add additional words. The first one has been done for you.

a I/write/complain/air-conditioning.
I'm writing to complain about our air-conditioning.
....

....

b I/expect/you/keep to/agreement.
....

....

c You/promise/arrange/somebody/come round/fix it.
....

....

d If/not send/someone/immediately/I/force/withhold/my rent/and/I/contact/the local council/complain.
....

....

e I/look forward/hear/you/soon.
....

....

f I try/call/tell you/air-conditioner/broken/but/you/not home.
....

....

g One of the reasons/I/decide/rent/apartment/because/air-conditioning.
....

....

B Complete this sample letter with sentences a–g on the previous page.

> Dear Mr Jones,
>
> **1** ..... , which has now been broken for over three weeks.
>
> I rent Unit 3C in Brown Street from you. On the 21st June, **2** ..... When I finally got in touch with you, **3** ..... It has been three weeks and nothing has been done about the problem. As you are aware, we are now in the middle of July and the temperatures recently have been very hot. **4** .....
>
> I can't concentrate with such high temperatures and this makes studying extremely difficult.
>
> As you will recall, the rental agreement states that you would deal with this kind of problem 'in a prompt and timely manner'. **5** ..... **6** .....
>
> **7** ..... .
>
> Yours,
>
> Bill Adams

> **express tip**
>
> In your letter of complaint, write three main paragraphs – one for each bullet point in the task.

3 Writing a letter of complaint

Before the task

A Read the question below and try to imagine the situation. Think about what additional information you will include. Underline the keywords in the question.

B Plan your letter in three paragraphs, with each paragraph addressing one of the points in the question.

Task practice

You should spend about 20 minutes on this task.

> *You recently took a trip with a taxi company. The driver behaved in an unacceptable way and you had a lot of problems. You complained to the company but no-one has replied to your complaint.*
>
> *Write a letter to the taxi company. In your letter*
> * *say why you are writing and how you feel*
> * *explain what happened*
> * *tell them what you would like them to do.*

Write at least 150 words.

You do **NOT** need to write any addresses.

Begin your letter as follows:

Dear ...,

Follow up

Read your letter again to check your spelling and grammar. Make sure that you have written at least 150 words.

Writing a General Training Essay

1 Planning your essay

A Read the General Training Task 2 question below and decide whether the sentences that follow are true (T) or false (F).

It is often said that children's leisure activities should be educational.
What kinds of activities can children learn from? Why should leisure activities be educational?
Give reasons for your answer and include any relevant examples from your experience.

1 You should say if you agree or disagree with the first sentence. .....
2 There are three points to address in this question. .....
3 You should list educational activities in your essay in bullet form. .....
4 You should give your opinion and some reasons. .....
5 You should talk about your favourite leisure activities as a child. .....

B The question asks 'What kinds of activities can children learn from?' Brainstorm a list of activities. In the second column write what children can learn from each one. Use note form.

Activity	Children can learn ...
reading	*to recognise words; to read more quickly; to enjoy books; about the world through fantasy or fiction.*

C The question above also asks 'Why should leisure activities be educational?' Look at the reasons below. Tick the ones you might include in this essay.
Children's leisure activities should be educational because ...
1 children have a lot to learn before they become adults.
2 learning through play helps prepare children for adult life.
3 playing with toys or games is a waste of time.
4 education is the most important thing in life.
5 educational activities can be fun as well as useful.
6 we don't live for long, so we should maximise every minute we have.

> **express tip**
> Follow an **A**, **B**, **C** procedure in the exam. **A**nalyse the question, **B**rainstorm ideas and **C**hoose your points.

D Add two more reasons of your own why children's leisure activities should be educational.
7 ....
8 ....

E Look again at the list of arguments above that you would include in your essay. Decide in which order you would use them in the essay. Decide how you would group your ideas into paragraphs.

2 | Writing an introduction to your essay

A The first paragraph of your essay should contain a restatement of the question in your own words. Here is the first sentence from the question again.

It is often said that children's leisure activities should be educational.

How could you say the following in a different way?

1 It is often said ....

2 children's leisure activities ....

3 should be educational ....

B Now write an opening sentence for your essay that restates the statement above in a different way.

....

C In the next sentence(s) of your introduction, you need to say how you will answer the question so that your reader knows what is coming in the rest of the essay. Read this example, then write your own sentences.

In this essay, I will give some examples of educational activities that are also fun and say what children can learn from them. Then, I will mention three main reasons why I believe it is important for leisure activities to be educational.

....

....

....

....

3 | Presenting opinions

Language bite

Presenting opinions

In the Task 2 essay, you are expected to present your personal opinion. In addition, you often need to present an opinion which is widely held by other people. The following expressions can be used:

Other people's opinions
It is often argued that ... ; Some people say that ...; Others believe that ...;

Personal opinions
In my personal opinion, ...; To my mind, ...; I tend to think that ...; I generally agree that ...; I believe that ...; Personally, I think ...

A Complete this extract from a sample essay using phrases from the **Language bite.**

.... *we should provide guided activities for young people so that they can learn whilst playing instead of allowing them to waste time undirected.*

.... *modern society places too much emphasis on examinations, creating stress for our young and not giving them the chance to simply 'be children' and play.*

.... *play should feature mostly guided activities, but there should also be opportunity for free activities.*

B Use your own ideas about the exam question in 1A above to complete these sentences.

Many people believe that ....

I personally think that ....

4 Concluding your essay

Language *bite*

Expressions for summarising

The final paragraph of your essay should be a conclusion in which you briefly restate your main arguments. The following expressions can be used in your concluding paragraph:

In short; In summary; To conclude; In conclusion; To sum up; Overall

A Read this example conclusion and then write your own, using the arguments you came up with earlier.

In summary, I personally believe that most leisure activities that children engage in should have some educational value. There are several reasons for this, including my belief that children need to be constantly learning plus the need for them to practise for real life. Overall, I think the most important thing is to get a balance between fun and serious activities so that children enjoy their childhood.

.... I believe that ....
.... There are
several reasons for this, ...
....
.... Overall, I think the most important reason is ....
....

5 Writing a General Training Essay

Before the task

A Read the question below. Underline the keywords.

B Brainstorm a list of arguments you want to include in your essay, and think of examples you can use to support your arguments.

C Choose the order in which you want to present your arguments, and decide how you will group them together into paragraphs.

Task practice

You should spend about 40 minutes on this task.

Write about the following topic:

It is generally agreed that we should take care of people in our community who are not able to do so themselves such as the poor, the elderly or the handicapped.

How can we help these people and why is it our responsibility?

Give reasons for your answer and include any relevant examples from your own knowledge or experience.

Write at least 250 words.

Follow up

Read your essay again to check the spelling and grammar. Make sure that you have written at least 250 words.

> **express tip**
>
> In the exam, you should not express your ideas in exactly the same way in the main body of the essay and the conclusion, so try to rephrase the main ideas in the conclusion.

1 Identifying stages in a process

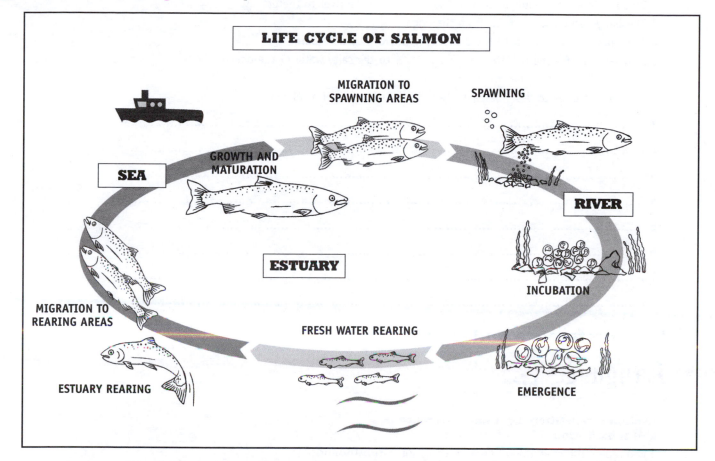

LIFE CYCLE OF SALMON

MIGRATION TO SPAWNING AREAS

SPAWNING

GROWTH AND MATURATION

SEA

RIVER

ESTUARY

INCUBATION

MIGRATION TO REARING AREAS

FRESH WATER REARING

ESTUARY REARING

EMERGENCE

A In Academic Writing Task 1 you may be asked to describe a process, for example, how something is made, or as in the diagram above, a cycle.

1 Look at the diagram above. What does it show? ....
2 How many stages are there in the life cycle above? ....
3 If you were describing this life cycle to someone, at which stage would you begin your description? ....

2 Describing a process

A Use the correct form of words from the labels on the diagram above to match the definitions below.

1 large amount of saltwater ....
2 the place where a river meets the sea or ocean ....
3 inland water such as lakes or rivers ....
4 young person or animal/fish/bird ....
5 release eggs into water ....
6 become an adult or fully grown ....
7 increase in size ....
8 come out of something ....
9 move from one place to another (animals, birds, fish) ....
10 become used to something ....

> **express tip**
>
> If it isn't clear where the process begins and ends (for example, a cycle), choose a logical beginning and start the process from there.

B Look at each stage of the process and decide what verbs you would need to describe it. Then complete the sentences with a verb in the present simple tense.

1 The baby salmon .... into adult salmon.

2 When they are big enough, they .... from the river to the estuary.

3 The baby fish .... from the eggs.

4 The salmon .... to the same river where they were born.

5 It takes time for the fish to .... to the salty water of the ocean.

C Write one sentence to describe each stage in the life cycle of a salmon.

1 ....

2 ....

3 ....

4 ....

5 ....

6 ....

7 ....

8 ....

3 Using reference and substitution

Language bite

Avoiding repetition by using reference and substitution

If you repeat the main noun all the time in your essay, it will sound repetitive. You can add variety to your writing by using reference and substitution, or other words/phrases instead of repeating 'the salmon'.

pronouns
it, they, these, those

substitution
the one(s), the one(s) that .... , the biggest/smallest one(s)

synonyms
the fish, the creature, the baby fish, the young fish, the juveniles, the adult fish

A Read this beginning of a description of the life cycle of a salmon. Replace the words in bold to avoid repetition.

The life cycle of a salmon begins and ends in the river and usually takes two to three years.

1 The salmon spawn or release eggs into the river. **2 The salmon** emerge from the eggs.

3 The salmon are not yet fully formed.

1 .... 2 .... 3 ....

B Reread the sentences you wrote in 2C to describe the life cycle of a salmon. Identify any places where you could use reference or substitution to avoid repetition and rewrite the sentences.

1 ....

2 ....

3 ....

4 ....

5 ....

6 ....

7 ....

8 ....

4 Linking your ideas

Language bite

Sequencers

When writing a process, it is important to use sequence words to show what order the events happened. Here are some examples of sequencers:

at the beginning of a process or cycle
first, first of all

in the middle
then, next, after that, following that

for the last stage
finally, at the end of the process

to mean 'from the moment when'
as soon as, once, immediately

A Look at this example of a writer combining sentences using sequencers. Note how the writer doesn't repeat the noun 'salmon' too many times.
The salmon spawn or release eggs into the river.
The salmon emerge from the eggs.
The salmon are not yet fully formed.
The adult salmon spawn or release the eggs into the river. After the incubation period, the baby fish emerge from the eggs but they are not yet fully formed.

Use linking phrases to connect these three sentences.
The salmon spend some time in the estuary. They move to the ocean. They migrate back up the estuary to the river.

....

....

B Go back to the list of sentences you wrote in 3B and combine them to create a complete essay describing the life cycle of a salmon.

> **express tip**
>
> Finish your essay at the same stage in the cycle from which you started. You could use the phrase '... *and here the cycle begins again*'.

5 Academic Writing Task 1: Describing a process

Before the task

A Look at the diagram below and decide how many stages there are. Decide which of those stages will come first in your description.

B Read the labels describing the stages and identify what the verb is each time. For those labels without a verb, decide what the verb should be.

C Decide how you will divide your essay into paragraphs. Which stages can be combined into a single paragraph?

Task practice

You should spend 20 minutes on this task.

The diagram below show shows the life cycle of a sea turtle.

Summarise the information by selecting and reporting the main features, and make comparisons where relevant.

Write at least 150 words.

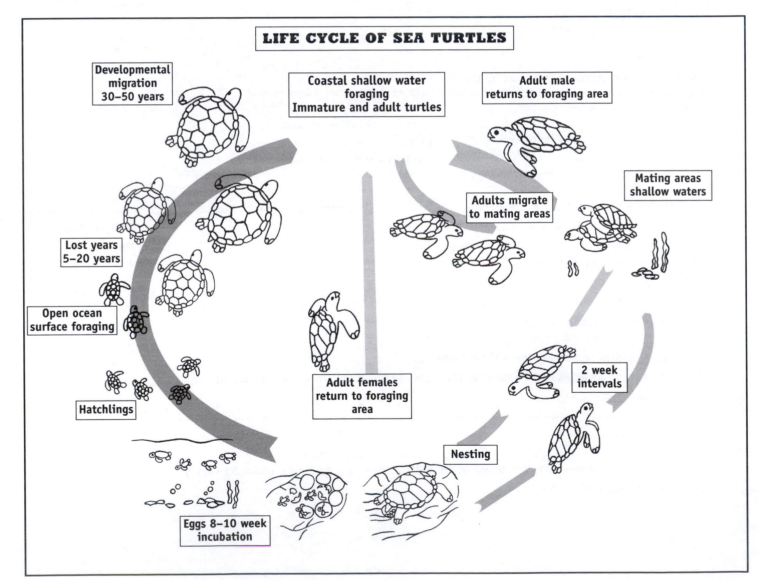

LIFE CYCLE OF SEA TURTLES

1 Studying Overseas

READING

2 Predicting content
A Topics 1, 4 and 6 will be mentioned in the article.

3 Matching statements to options
Task practice

1 Answer: A
Note 'In tutorials, you are expected to be much more active – asking questions and giving your opinions – and I found it very difficult at first.'

2 Answer: B
Note 'Another problem for me was reading. It was very hard at first to read long texts in English.'

3 Answer: C
Note '... I was too worried about making mistakes ...'

4 Answer: A
Note 'In my opinion, it's not just your level of English that you need to work on – it's your approach to studying in general.'

5 Answer: B
Note 'If you want my advice, take a preparation course before you start your main degree'.

6 Answer: B
Note 'We were shown techniques to improve our reading ... now I feel a lot more confident about reading in English ...'

7 Answer: C
Note 'What I found very hard was taking part in discussions ... and I knew enough about the topics ...'

8 Answer: C
Note 'My advice to students is make sure your English level is high enough before you go overseas ...'

4 Skimming and scanning
A b; C 1 China; 2 Muslim cultures; 3 three times

5 True/False/Not Given
Before the task
1 A; 2 A; 3 A; 4 B; 5 B; 6 B; 7 C; 8 C

Task practice

1 Answer: True
Note '... people might be understanding if you have troubles with their language ...'

2 Answer: False
Note '... they are less likely to be forgiving if you break the unwritten social rules.'

3 Answer: True
Note '... in Japan it is considered rude to blow your nose in public ...'

4 Answer: True
Note 'The best advice we can give you is to learn some of the local customs of the people you will be spending time with.'

5 Answer: Not Given
Note There is no mention of using chopsticks with your left hand.

6 Answer: Not Given
Note There is no mention of how many courses there are in an Italian meal.

7 Answer: True
Note '... they might consider you impolite if you use your left.'

8 Answer: False
Note 'In Britain, shaking hands is mainly done between men ...'

6 Short-answer questions
Before the task
A 9 what; 10 what; 11 what; 12 who; 13 how many
B 9 A; 10 B; 11 C; 12 C; 13 C

Task practice

9 Answer: your (cotton) handkerchief
Note '... heaven forbid you put your cotton handkerchief back in your pocket! ...'

10 Answer: a second plateful
Note '... so never refuse a second plateful!'

11 Answer: a business card
Note 'If you are given a business card in ... Singapore, and you don't accept it in both hands, you'll be showing disrespect ...'

12 Answer: men
Note 'In Britain, shaking hands is mainly done between men ...'

13 Answer: twice
Note 'The Italians kiss ... it's twice – once on each cheek ...'

VOCABULARY

1 Word building

A

noun	verb	adjective	adverb
expectation	expect	expected	expectedly
completion	complete	complete	completely
analysis	analyse	analytical	analytically
construction	construct	constructive	constructively
introduction	introduce	introductory	
appreciation	appreciate	appreciative	appreciatively
sympathy	sympathise	sympathetic	sympathetically
satisfaction	satisfy	satisfied/ satisfying	satisfactorily/ satisfyingly
society	socialise	social	socially
comfort	comfort	comfortable	comfortably

B 1 constructive; **2** analytical; **3** appreciative; **4** sympathise; **5** completing

2 Vocabulary in context

A 1 tutorial; **2** assignment; **3** topic; **4** support; **5** approach; **6** argument; **7** text; **8** degree; **9** challenge; **10** style

B 1 format; **2** appendix; **3** prioritise; **4** reduce; **5** text; **6** theme; **7** project; **8** criteria; **9** draft; **10** abstract

C noun only: abstract, appendix, criteria, theme, text; **verb only:** prioritise, reduce; **noun or verb:** draft, format, project

SPEAKING

1 Talking about likes and dislikes

A Suggested order: hate/can't stand, dislike/don't like, don't mind, like/enjoy/(be) fond of, really like, love

B Answers will vary.

2 Talking about travelling abroad

A Speaker 1 likes travelling abroad; Speaker 2 dislikes travelling abroad.

B Speaker 1 likes travelling by plane, the whole experience of a new culture and meeting new people; Speaker 2 dislikes foreign food and being in a tiny space for hours and hours.

3 Talking about where you come from

B See listening script for details.

4 Talking about plans for the future

A 1 go abroad and have a holiday; **2** continue studies in Canada and become a doctor; **3** study at Exeter University; **4** study law in the United States; **5** move to New Zealand

B 1 I'm planning to ...; **2** I'm probably going to ...; **3** I'm hoping to ...; **4** I'd really love to ...; **5** I'm definitely going to ...

2 Shopping and the Internet

LISTENING

1 Introduction

A 1 dollar; **2** euro; **3** pound; **4** cent; **5** pence or pee

B 1 $20; **2** before; **3** after; **4** 50¢, **5** 75p

C 1 sixty-five dollars; **2** eight hundred and fifty pounds; **3** one thousand four hundred euros, or fourteen hundred euros; **4** ten thousand dollars; **5** one million pounds, or a million pounds; **6** six dollars fifty; **7** ten pounds ninety-nine; **8** ninety cents; **9** twenty-five pence, or twenty-five pee; **10** fifteen euros

D 1 $350; **2** £50,000; **3** €15,000; **4** $5.50; **5** 80p

2 Predicting what you will hear

A 1 a name; **2** a place; **3** a number; **4** a number; **5** a place

B 1 sea; **2** pool; **3** 4/four; **4** 300; **5** the Internet

C 1 a number; **2** a plural noun; **3** a name; **4** a number; **5** a name

D 1 35; **2** songs; **3** cable; **4** 200; **5** telephone

3 Notes completion

Before the task

Answer 5 is probably a number; 1 (and possibly 2) might be a name.

Task practice

1 underwater; **2** (scuba) divers; **3** (really) light; **4** can of drink; **5** forty/40

4 Form completion

Task practice

1 Gerrard; **2** 129; **3** 4010; **4** 038164572; **5** July 1st; **6** (the) pen; **7** credit card; **8** (a) friend

VOCABULARY

1 Word building
A

verb	noun	antonym verb
sell	sale	buy
save	savings	spend
profit	profit	lose
rise	rise	fall
lend	loan	borrow
increase	increase	decrease
withdraw	withdrawal	deposit

B 1 The TV *cost* a lot of money.
2 The banks *raised* the interest rate again last month.
3 My father *lent* me the money to buy a car.
4 I *withdrew* £300 from the bank this morning.
5 Over 50% of the price of a CD goes to the record company as *profit*.

2 Vocabulary in context
A 1 S; **2** S; **3** H; **4** H; **5** H; **6** S; **7** H; **8** S; **9** H; **10** S; **11** H; **12** H
B 1 borrow; **2** lend; **3** owed; **4** overdrawn; **5** spends **6** bankrupt

WRITING

1 Using fractions and percentages
A 1 e; **2** c; **3** f; **4** a; **5** d; **6** b
B 1 one/a sixth; **2** one/a tenth; **3** four fifths; **4** a/one fifth; **5** two eighths **6** two and a half

C 1 two out of three; **2** one in ten; **3** 99%; **4** one in ten; **5** two out of three; **6** 26%; **7** 26%; **8** 99%
D 1 approximately half; almost half; nearly 50%; just under half; **2** 80%, four fifths, four out of five; **3** a third, one in three; **4** a sixth; **5** one hundredth, one percent; **6** four out of a hundred, fewer than one in twenty, one in twenty-five

2 Interpreting data
A 1 F – not 'most' accidents (that would mean over 50% but it is only 16%). The biggest single cause is looking at a crash, roadside incident or traffic; **2** T; **3** T; **4** F – almost one in ten; **5** T
B 1 cause; **2** are caused; **3** caused; **4** causes; **5** are caused

3 Making comparisons
A 1 less; **2** fewer; **3** more; **4** fewer; **5** less
B 1 less, fewer; **2** fewer, bigger; **3** fewer, lesser; **4** less, fewer; **5** less, bigger
C 1 cheaper; **2** The highest; **3** Fewer; **4** The biggest; **5** the most successful

4 Expressing similarities and differences
A talking about similarities: both, also, and, as ... as, have in common, similar, the same as;
talking about differences: although, even though, however, not as ... as, whereas, while
B 1 both; **2** Even though; **3** whereas; **4** in common.

5 Describing charts
See model answer on page 93.

3 Jobs and Job-hunting

READING

2 Identifying keywords and paraphrasing
A 1 trendy; **2** opportunities; **3** workforce; **4** discrimination; **5** deal with; **6** suffer; **7** absence; **8** flourished; **9** Suggested answers: accountant, flight attendant, teacher; **10** policies

3 Matching information to sections of text
Task practice

1 Answer: D

Note '... the financial services industry, the airlines industry and the independent schooling system.'

2 Answer: A

Note '... as our lives have become more complex, expensive or stressful and as we demand more ...'

3 Answer: C

Note 'Job-sharing has been seen as a cure for such economic problems as unemployment ...'

4 Answer: C

Note 'The rewards for the employee are ... it is especially popular with women nearing the end of their pregnancies ...'

5 Answer: D

Note 'Indeed, the school system has played a pioneering role with regard to flexible work practices.'

6 Answer: B

Note 'In 1998, The Human Rights and Equal Opportunities Commission made a landmark decision ...'

4 Reading for gist
A 1 a; **2** b

5 Sentence completion

Task practice

1 F; 2 C; 3 E; 4 role reversal; 5 highly-educated women;
6 self-esteem; 7 guilt

VOCABULARY

1 Word building

A

verb	noun thing	noun person	adjective
train	training	trainer/trainee	trained
employ	employment	employer/employee	employed
	unemployment		unemployed
apply	application	applicant	
interview	interview	interviewer/interviewee	
qualify	qualification		qualified

B 1 qualified/trained; 2 application; 3 interview;
4 unemployed; 5 qualifications; 6 employment;
7 applicants; 8 training; 9 unemployment;
10 qualify

2 Vocabulary in context

A 1 salary; 2 employed; 3 compensation;
4 full-time; 5 experience; 6 income; 7 qualification;
8 contract; 9 uniform; 10 promotion; 11 training;
12 application

SPEAKING

1 Using notes to organise your Part 2 talk

B 1 Yes; 2 Yes; 3 Yes; 4 past tense – because the
interview happened in the past and is finished.

C Extra details include: her university studies, her
knowledge of computers

2 Talking about jobs

A c

Crime and Punishment

4

LISTENING

1 Introduction

A 1 prisoner; 2 criminal; 3 suspect; 4 accused

B suggested order: a 1; b 10; c 8; d 2; e 6; f 5;
g 3; h 9; i 4; j 7

2 Identifying synonyms and paraphrasing

A 1 Identify theft; 2 much later; 3 protect yourself

B 1 it is called identity theft; 2 realise; 3 have been the
victim; 4 much later; 5 minimise the chance/know how
to protect

3 Predicting what you will hear

A b pretending to be another person; d getting access to
someone's personal information

B 1 B; 2 B

C 1 Why not A? This is an example of identity theft not
the definition of it;
Why not C? This sounds like the answer but doesn't
really explain what identity theft means as a crime. Look
at the listening script for part 2 and see how the words
in B mean the same thing.
2 The listening script says 'new technologies' so A is
mentioned using different words.; The listening script
says 'the growth in international trade' which is the
same meaning as C. The word 'growth' is used and
'crime' in the same sentence but it does not say that all
crimes have increased so B is NOT given as a reason.

4 Notes completion

Task practice

1 driving licence; 2 documents; 3 cheques/checks;
4 computer

5 Short-answer questions

Task practice

5 (your) security awareness; 6 (a) password;
7 personal details; 8 secure websites;
9 (your) bank

Follow-up

B possible answers: crime, theft, victim, criminal,
illegally, commit (a crime), thief, steal, stolen, burglary,
fraud, hacker, break into, illegal, report

6 Multiple-choice questions

Task practice

1 B; 2 C; 3 A; 4 A

VOCABULARY

1 Word building

A

Crime	Person	Verb form(s)
burglary	burglar	burgle commit a burglary
kidnapping	kidnapper	kidnap
murder	murderer	murder commit a murder
arson	arsonist	commit arson set fire to something
vandalism	vandal	vandalise
theft	thief	(steal)
shoplifting	shoplifter	steal something from a shop
robbery	robber	rob

B 1 robbery; 2 arson; 3 murder; 4 burglary; 5 vandalism; 6 kidnapping; 7 theft

2 Vocabulary in context

A 1 f; 2 h; 3 d; 4 a; 5 b; 6 e; 7 c; 8 g

B 1 electronic tagging; 2 fine; 3 suspended sentence; 4 execution; 5 caning; 6 stoning; 7 community service

WRITING

1 Seeing two sides of an argument

C a F; b F; c A; d F; e A; f A

D Suggested ideas:

Statement 2

For:

a We should not use violence to provide entertainment.

b It gives people the mistaken idea that society is violent and unsafe.

c People, especially children, mimic the behaviour they see on television.

Against:

a Viewers know the difference between fictionalised violence and the real thing.

b TV Channels indicate to viewers if a programme contains violence, so parents can choose to switch off.

c These programmes are not shown in the early evening, when younger children may be watching television.

Statement 3

For:

a The police should be equipped to deal with modern criminals.

b If the police are well-trained, there should be little risk.

c Knowing the police are armed is a deterrent to criminals.

Against:

a Most crime is non-violent and doesn't require an armed response by the police.

b We don't want anyone, neither the police nor criminals, to bring weapons into the community.

c If criminals know the police have guns, they think that they should also carry weapons.

2 Planning and organising your essay

A Answers will vary.

B Answers will vary.

3 Using linking expressions

A 1 b; 2 c; 3 f; 4 g; 5 a; 6 e; 7 d

B what's more; show a contrast: but, however; show a consequence: so; express an opinion: it is clear to me that, it seems to me that; give a reason: because; give an example: after all, for example; list a sequence of events: finally, next, secondly, then

4 Showing contrast

A 1 despite/in spite of; 2 even though; 3 However, 4 Although

B 1 It seems to me that; 2 Therefore; 3 Furthermore; 4 after all; 5 In my view

This paragraph is for the statement.

5 Writing a 'for and against' essay

See model answer on page 93.

5 | Transport and Inventions

READING

2 Predicting Content

A 1 F; 2 F; 3 T

B 'In this article, we take a look at this form of transport (mass transit railways) in three South East Asian cities: Bangkok, Kuala Lumpur and Singapore.'

3 Building a map of the text

A The passage is organised by categories

B The three sections are: Bangkok, Kuala Lumpur and Singapore

C b

D Suggested answers:

B The Bangkok project had a number of problems.

C The Sky Train is having trouble attracting customers.

D Kuala Lumpur's system faced financial difficulties.

E The LRT relies on technology to improve safety.

F The new MRT line in Singapore is automated.

G Singapore encourages public transport use by linking different types.

4 Matching headings to paragraphs

Task practice

A ix; **B** vii; **C** vi; **D** viii; **E** i; **F** v; **G** iv

5 Multiple-choice questions

Task practice

1 Answer: D

Note '... was reluctant to invest public funds ...'

2 Answer: C

Note '... a taxi driver was killed ...'

3 Answer: A

Note '... the Sky Train opened ahead of schedule.'

4 Answer: A

Note ' ... there is a further challenge for the operators: persuading people to use the system.'

5 Answer: C
Note 'Although construction had already been completed ...'
6 Answer: A
Note 'At present, around 10,000 people ride the train daily, but the target figure is 30,000.'
7 Answer: A
Note 'In terms of safety, passengers can communicate directly with the control centre ...'
8 Answer: A
Note 'Adding to Singapore's existing Mass Rapid Transport ...'
9 Answer: A and B;
10 Answer: B and C

VOCABULARY

1 Word building

A

verb	noun
reduce	reduction
communicate	communication
intrude	intrusion
detect	detection
extend	extension
integrate	integration
construct	construction
automate	automation
implement	implementation
combine	combination

B 1 construct; **2** reduce; **3** automate; **4** intrude;
  5 combine; **6** integrate; **7** extend; **8** detect;
  9 communicate; **10** implement

2 Vocabulary in context

A 1 communication; **2** intrusion; **3** detect,
  4 combination; **5** automated; **6** reduce
B 1 threats; **2** prevent; **3** external; **4** expertise;
  5 secure; **6** fully; **7** overall; **8** costs

SPEAKING

1 Giving your opinion
A 1 CP; **2** PT; **3** PT; **4** CP

2 Agreeing and disagreeing
A 1 2; **2** 1; **3** 5; **4** 4; **5** 3
B Speaker 1 PA; **Speaker 2** D; **Speaker 3** A
C 2
Agreeing: I absolutely agree
Disagreeing: I don't agree at all; I don't think so
Partly Agreeing: I agree up to a point; I agree with you to an extent

3 Expressing levels of certainty
A 1 could, may not; **2** might, could; **3** will, won't, should

6 The Natural World

LISTENING

1 Introduction
A 1 g; **2** b; **3** c; **4** d; **5** f; **6** a; **7** e

2 Identifying speakers and attitude
A 1 male, low; **2** female, high; **3** male, high
B interest Oh, sounds great, Wow, that's interesting;
  confusion Sorry, I don't know what you mean,
  I don't follow you;
  agreement Yes, that's right, Exactly.

3 Classification

Task practice

1 D; **2** C; **3** C; **4** A; **5** B

Follow up

Surprise: Wow, no way! You're kidding!
Understanding: Oh, I get it. Mm, I see.

4 Table completion

Task practice

6 100; **7** 10; **8** crater; **9** Japan; **10** 300;
11 steep slopes; **12** secondary cones

5 Notes completion

Before the task

1 conservation; **2** mammal; **3** naturalist; **4** extinction;
5 endangered; **6** biodiversity

Task practice

1 Frozen Ark; **2** life codes; **3** 25; **4** ecosystem;
5 genetic information; **6** database

6 Summary completion

Task practice

7 tissue samples; **8** insect; **9** low temperatures;
10 clone

VOCABULARY

1 Word building

A increase: shoot up, grow, rise, soar, rocket;
  decrease: plummet, plunge, crash, fall, decline, drop;
  go up and down: fluctuate;
  stay the same: stabilise, level off;
  large: significant, considerable, sizable, remarkable, major;
  small: faint, slight, mild, gentle, minor
B 1 plummeted; **2** considerably; **3** levelling off;
  4 fluctuate; **5** shot up

2 Vocabulary in context

1 fell/dropped/decreased; **2** steadily/continuously;
3 dived/plunged/dropped/crashed; **4** fall/decrease;
5 a low/a low point; **6** rise/increase; **7** fluctuated;
8 shot up/rocketed/soared; **9** high/peak; **10** slight/minor;
11 drop/fall; **12** rise/increase

WRITING

1 Identifying trends

A a, d, e, show trends; b, c, f do not
B 1 F – The graph shows the percentage of fatal shark attacks, Not the number of people or the number of attacks. Look at the vertical axis.; **2** T; **3** T; **4** F – Luxembourg had the highest GDP with about 44 thousand dollars per capita in 2001. (Notice the vertical axis is thousands of dollars). **5** T; **6** F – The graph provides no specific information about Europe.

2 Writing introductory statements

A 1 1, 3, 5 are introductory sentences.
2 shows
B Suggested answers:
graph e: The bar chart shows the changes in global oil consumption every five years from 1980 to 2050.
graph f: The bar chart shows the location, date and magnitude of the world's five worst earthquakes.

3 Academic Writing Task 1: Describing a graph

Before the task

One possible introductory sentence:
The line graph shows the increase in concentrations of atmospheric carbon dioxide for the period 1850 to 2050.

Task practice

See model answer on page 93.

4 Academic Writing Task 1: Describing a table

Before the task

1 T; **2** F (The number of bird species decreased from 67 to 44 during this period); **3** F (there is no information about this in the table); **4** T; **5** T (from 15% to 50%).

Task practice

See model answer on page 93.

7 Food and Diet

READING

2 Identifying the writer's opinion

A i Not Given; **ii** Yes; **iii** No
B 1 Yes '... one in four children is overweight or obese and, for boys, this figure rises to one in three.'; **2** Not Given – it only says that overweight boys are more sedentary than girls.

3 Yes/No/Not Given

Task practice

1 Answer: Yes

Note 'The majority of children were found to be quite knowledgeable about nutrition.'

2 Answer: No

Note '... many children were aware that foods ... such as sweets and fast food could be eaten occasionally, but not every day.'

3 Answer: No

Note '... the recommended sixty minutes or more of exercise.'

4 Answer: No

Note 'Whilst ... health education programs seem to be having some success in ... nutrition, the children seem to have problems utilising this knowledge to maintain a normal healthy weight.'

5 Answer: Yes

Note '... children replied that homework and a lack of time were the biggest problems ...'

6 Answer: Not Given

Note There is no mention in the passage of infectious diseases.

7 Answer: Yes

Note 'These patterns mirror similar trends in other parts of the world.'

8 Answer: No

Note Cars are only one of several examples given, all of which are contributing to obesity.

9 Answer: Not Given

Note The article doesn't confirm or deny this.

10 Answer: Not Given

Note Although the passage says that children like their parents to watch them play sports, there is no mention of how many parents actually do so.

4 Classification

Task practice

11 Answer: D

Note 'These patterns mirror similar trends in other parts of the world.'

12 Answer: C

Note '... mounting evidence that the worldwide rise in obesity levels is due to falling levels of physical activity.'

13 Answer: A

Note '... families and schools must be involved in encouraging ...'

14 Answer: B

Note '... ninety percent of the children surveyed reported ...'

15 Answer: C

Note '... life based on countless labour-saving devices ...'

5 Summary completion

Task practice

16 nutrition; **17** overweight boys; **18** physical exercise; **19** education programmes; **20** leisure time; **21** globalisation; **22** inspiration; **23** enjoyment; **24** cooperation; **25** participation

VOCABULARY

1 Word Building

A show: claim, report, reveal, suggest, confirm, find, indicate;
study: research, investigate, examine, look into, consider, explore;
research: study, investigation, survey, inquiry;
results: evidence, findings, facts, proof, confirmation, support;
people who do research: investigator, researcher, academic, expert

B 2 discovery; **3** expert; **4** make; **5** inquire; **6** knowledge

2 Vocabulary in context

Suggested answers: 1 results/findings; **2** study/ investigation; **3** investigated/looked into; **4** findings/results; **5** published; **6** Researchers; **7** evidence; **8** found/discovered; **9** revealed/found; **10** fact

SPEAKING

1 Structuring your talk

C Order of points: Speaker 1: what, when, why, where, who cooks, how; **Speaker 2:** when, what, how, who cooks, where, why

D 1 simple present;
2 Speaker 1: I'm going to talk about the meal we usually eat at Christmas in my country. **Speaker 2:** I'd like to tell you about something special we eat in Germany.
3 Speaker 1: I love Christmas Dinner – it's my favourite meal of the whole year. **Speaker 2:** I love Easter eggs as they remind me of happy times with my family when I was young.

8 Sickness and Health

LISTENING

1 Introduction

A parts of the body: gallbladder, intestines, kidney, liver; lungs, blood, immune system, stomach, digestive system; **health and sickness:** cure, injury, recover, symptom, discomfort, treatment, illness, pain; **food and diet:** vitamins, nutrients, minerals

2 Recognising signposts

A a 3; **b** 4; **c** 7; **d** 1; **e** 6; **f** 2; **g** 8; **h** 5;
B 1 c; **2** b; **3** h; **4** d; **5** e; **6** c; **7** g; **8** e; **9** d; **10** d; **11** g; **12** a; **13** a; **14** a; **15** c; **16** c; **17** g; **18** b; **19** h; **20** f; **21** f; **22** h; **23** d; **24** d; **25** e; **26** e

3 Notes completion

Task practice

1 2.5; **2** main filter; **3** nutrients; **4** (potentially) dangerous; **5** medicines; **6** extra blood; **7** energy

Follow up

1 for example; **2** although; **3** Not only that

4 Labelling a diagram

Task practice

8 liver; **9** stomach; **10** break down food; **11** cause blockages; **12** small intestine

Follow up

Let's move on to look at ...

5 Multiple-choice

Task practice

13 C, D; **14** B; **15** B; **16** A

Follow up

Before we finish today ...

VOCABULARY

1 Word building

A

verb	noun
prevent	prevention
treat	treatment
insure	insurance
detect	detection
recover	recovery
eradicate	eradication
remove	removal
suffer	suffering
operate	operation
reduce	reduction
produce	production
avoid	avoidance
cure	cure
medicate	medication
occur	occurrence
absorb	absorption
include	inclusion

B 1 recovering; **2** eradicate; **3** insurance; **4** avoid;
5 treatment

2 Vocabulary in context

1 treatment; **2** medication; **3** detected/treated;
4 cured/eradicated; **5** prevented; **6** avoid; **7** operation;
8 recovery; **9** suffering; **10** production

WRITING

1 Brainstorming arguments for and against

A Suggested answers:

Vegetarians can't eat: meat, fish, chicken, shellfish, insects, etc.

Vegetarians can eat: any vegetable, fruit, grain, seed, nut, etc. dairy products, eggs.

Vegans can't eat: as well as anything vegetarians can't eat, dairy products, eggs, honey

B Possible answers: 1 health issues; ethical/religious issues; environmental issues; **2** health issues; people are designed to eat meat; people owe no obligations to animals/animals have no special rights

2 Deciding your main ideas

C 1 agree; **2 a** health issues, **b** ethical/religious arguments, **c** environmental factors
E Yes.

3 Structuring an agree or disagree essay

A 1 e; **2** d; **3** a; **4** c; **5** b
B Used to present examples: one example in the UK was; including; for instance; A well-documented problem is; for example; **Used to introduce an opinion:** I personally believe; I ... believe the benefits ...
C 1 however; **2** including; **3** For instance; **4** However; **5** one example; **6** Another reason for

4 Writing Task 2: Agree or disagree essay

See model answer on page 94.

General Training 1A: Writing a Letter of Request

1 Understanding the question

A

	sender	receiver	level of formality	type of request
a	student	English school administration	F	information
b	student	college lecturer	F/SF	permission
c	tenant	agency	F	permission
d	friend	friend	I	favour

B b key words in situation: taking a course, deadline, project, last week, haven't finished
   verbs in task: write; introduce; explain; request
c Key words in situation: renting a flat, agency, contract, one year, need to leave, four months early
   verbs in task: write, introduce, ask, explain
d key words in situation: parents, arriving, working at the time; **verbs in task:** write, explain, ask, offer

2 Using appropriate language and organisation

A 1 As you know, As I'm sure you are aware;
  2 Unfortunately, I'm afraid that; **3** I was wondering if you could, I would be extremely grateful if you could;
  4 I realise that, I understand that, I'm aware that;
  5 I hope you can understand my situation, Yours faithfully, I look forward to hearing from you soon.
B The answer to all the questions is 'yes'.
C Dear Ms McCall
   My name is Cao Ying and I am a first year student in your E3K (biology) class at Shafton College.
   I am writing to you because I have a problem with the project you set about life cycles. The due date was last week but I'm afraid I haven't finished it yet. As you know, I have been absent from class for almost ten days with glandular fever and I have not been attending lectures. I only managed to get the reading list from a friend and go to the library to do research yesterday.
   You will see from your records that I have never missed a deadline for an assignment so far during my course.

However, I am requesting an extension of one week in this case because I am so behind with my work. I hope you will take my illness into consideration and grant me an extension.
Yours sincerely
Cao Ying

3 Writing a letter of request

See model answer on page 94.

GT 1B: Writing a Letter of Complaint

1 Introducing a complaint

A a a tenant; **b** a landlord; **c** semi-formal

B I am writing to complain about our air-conditioning, which has now been broken for over three weeks.

C I am writing to complain about my TV, which has been broken for a week.

2 Describing your complaint

A b I expect you to keep our agreement.
  c You promised to arrange for somebody to come round to fix it.
  d If you don't send someone immediately, I will be forced to withhold my rent, and I will contact the local council to complain.
  e I look forward to hearing from you soon.
  f I tried to call to tell you the air-conditioner was broken, but you weren't home.
  g One of the reasons I decided to rent this apartment was because of the air-conditioning.

B1 a; **2** f; **3** c; **4** g; **5** b; **6** d; **7** e

3 Writing a letter of complaint

See model answer on page 94.

GT 2: Writing a General Training Essay

1 Planning your essay

A 1 F – it is not an agree/disagree essay. It is usually best to accept the first sentence as a fact and address the question or statements that come after it.
  2 F – two main parts: what ...? Why ...?
  3 F – Never put lists in bullet points in the essay, though this would be a useful way to plan.
  4 T – you must give reasons because the question asks you to.
  5 Could be either. This could be relevant if you use your personal experience as support for your main points.

2 Writing an introduction to your essay

A Possible answers: it is often said – many people believe; it is sometimes argued that children's leisure activities – the activities that children do in their free time; should be educational – need to have educational value.

B Possible answer: It is sometimes argued that children should engage in activities that have some educational value or benefit.

3 Presenting opinions

A It is often argued that, Some people say that; Others believe that, Personally, I believe that; In my personal opinion; I tend to think that.

4 Concluding your essay

Answers will vary.

5 Writing a General Training essay

See model answer on page 95.

Academic Writing: Describing a process

1 Identifying stages in a process

1 It shows the life cycle of a salmon; **2** eight; **3** Answers for this may vary, but one logical point would be the spawning of eggs and death of adult salmon.

2 Describing a process

A 1 ocean; **2** estuary; **3** freshwater; **4** juvenile; **5** spawn; **6** mature; **7** grow; **8** emerge; **9** migrate; **10** adapt

B Starting at the spawning and following around the cycle: spawn, die, emerge, grow, feed, migrate, adapt, return
  1 grow, mature, develop; **2** migrate; **3** emerge; **4** return; **5** adapt

C Possible answers:
Adult salmon spawn or release eggs into the river; Baby salmon emerge from eggs; They stay in freshwater to grow bigger, where they feed on insects; Juvenile salmon then migrate from the river to the estuary where fresh and salt water mix; This helps them adapt to the change in water before they move to the ocean; After spending some time in the estuary, the salmon migrate to the ocean where they can continue to grow in salt water; Here they feed and grow to mature adult size in the ocean where there is plenty of food; Once they are fully grown, many salmon migrate back up the estuary to the river to the spawning areas; The cycle starts again as the adults spawn and the next batch of eggs is ready; The salmon die soon after spawning.

3 Using reference and substitution

A Possible answers: 1 the adult fish; **2** the baby salmon; **3** the juveniles

4 Linking your ideas

A Sample answer:

First, the salmon spend some time in the estuary. Following this, they move to the ocean. Finally, they migrate back up the estuary to the river.

B Sample answer:

The life cycle of a salmon begins and ends in the river. First, the adult salmon releases eggs into the river, a process called spawning. When the baby fish emerge from the eggs, they are not yet fully formed, so they remain in the freshwater of the river until they grow bigger, feeding on insects. Next, the baby salmon migrate from the river to the estuary, or mouth of the river. This is where freshwater and saltwater mix. The juvenile fish spend some time here in order to adapt to the change in the water.

The salmon then move to the saltwater of the ocean, where they can continue to grow to a mature size. When they are fully mature, many of them migrate back up the estuary to the spawning areas.

5 Academic Writing Task 1: Describing a process
See model answer on page 95.

Model Writing Answers
Unit 2

5 Academic Writing Task 1: Describing charts

The bar chart shows mobile phone ownership based on gender in one university. The pie charts have information on the different phone operators used by these students. Out of a total student body of just under 9,000, the vast majority of people own mobile phones (8,653 out of a total of 8,900). When this number is divided by gender, we find only a narrow gap in ownership; in fact, the figure for male students is slightly higher than the females at 51% compared to 49%. Of the 247 students who do not own mobile phones, the percentage of males is almost double that of the females, with 163 and 84 respectively.

Turning to the pie charts, we can see that the three main telephone companies are Supafone, Phonefast and Mobicall. The first pie chart focuses on which companies the male students use and the figures for the three companies are very similar. Mobicall has the largest market share with 36%. Phonefast is only two percentage points behind at 34% and Supafone follows closely with 30%. In contrast, the figures for the female market are very different, with practically all women choosing either Supafone or Phonefast (40% and 45% respectively), whilst Mobicall's market share is significantly smaller at just 15%.

Unit 4

5 Writing a 'for and against' essay

'What a wicked web we weave, when first we practice to deceive.' This famous quotation means if you start with small lies, it is very possible that you will later have to tell bigger and bigger ones. Naturally, this is very dangerous because you might get yourself into all kinds of problems. I therefore think that it is better to avoid lying if you possibly can. The main reason I believe that lying is to be avoided is because relationships are built on trust and trust comes from honesty. By this I mean, whether you are a businessperson or a friend, we need to feel that we can rely on the other person to tell us truth and not try to deceive us. Indeed, it is deceitful if we lie to somebody else and we can lose that person's trust for ever.

Despite the arguments I have put forward in the preceding paragraph, I believe that there are situations where lying is more acceptable. I think the most common example of this is when it is necessary to either withhold the truth or tell a so-called 'white lie' in order to avoid upsetting someone's feelings. For instance, your friend might have bought a new dress and ask you how she looks. If you actually think that she looks terrible, you will probably decide not to tell the truth. Instead, you might say that the dress is unusual, or you might simply lie and say that your friend looks nice. I don't believe that this kind of untruth is wrong.

To sum up, the problem with not telling the truth is that it can damage relationships. However, there are occasions when telling a small lie is more acceptable in order to avoid hurting someone's feelings.

Unit 6

3 Academic Writing Task 1: Report
TASK A

The chart illustrates how much oil was consumed worldwide between 1980 and 2000. It is divided into seven regions and gives usage in thousands of barrels per day. In this twenty year period, two areas (North America and Western Europe) maintained a relatively stable level of consumption, although the American figure was substantially higher than the European figure (roughly 20,000 barrels compared to just over 10,000 barrels respectively). The other region which remained steady in terms of oil consumed was Africa, with the smallest number of barrels used - at just 2, 000 per day.

During the period, oil consumption in Eastern Europe dropped significantly from 10,000 to 3,000 barrels a day. The other areas (the Middle East, Central and South America and the Far East) all saw their consumption increase. The Far East experienced the greatest increase, doubling from approximately 10,000 barrels in 1980/85 to 20,000 in 2000. Central and South America consumed just over 3,000 barrels at the beginning of the period and, by the year 2000, was consuming just under 6,000 barrels of oil per day. The Middle East began with a figure of approximately 1,000 barrels, but increased steadily to finish with a consumption of 3,000 barrels a day.

Overall, oil consumption tended to increase in this period with the notable exception of Eastern Europe.

TASK B

The table shows the percentage change of several key indicators of a small island from 1980 to the present day. The first two factors are environmental: how much of the island is covered forest and the number of bird species. Both have seen significant decreases during this time. The number of bird species has dropped from 67 in 1980 to only 44 now. At the beginning of the period, 37% of the island was forested, yet only 17% now remains. Employment figures show similar dramatic changes, with the percentage of the population in the fishing industry falling from 80% to 30%, whilst the tourism sector saw the reverse, with figures of 15% growing steadily to 50% in the present day. Turning to social issues, we can see that the number of houses with running water and electricity has risen dramatically from zero to almost one hundred percent in this time frame. The percentage of children of school age attending school has improved significantly: starting with a third of the population in 1980, the figure more than doubled in 1995 and reached a high of 85% in the present day.

Overall, there have been many changes both environmentally and socially on this island between 1980 and the present day.

Unit 8

4 Academic Writing Task 2: 'Agree or disagree' essay

In an age of animal rights activists and environmentalism, the use of animals for testing purposes causes strong controversy. Some people argue that we must behave in a responsible and compassionate way towards the world around us. I tend to agree with this point of view, although I am still uncertain about the necessity for some kinds of testing.

The cosmetics industry is not recent; in fact, it has a history of thousands of years. Since there is a huge range of products already available, it is entirely unnecessary to test any more products on animals. Another reason against testing is that I find it difficult to accept the idea of animals being harmed or suffering simply to indulge human vanity.

Testing for drugs, on the other hand, is a more difficult ethical dilemma. Some people argue that it is necessary to use animals at certain stages of the development of medicines in order to avoid the risk of serious harm to humans. Whilst this might be true, I personally believe that medical knowledge is sufficiently advanced to make this type of testing no longer necessary.

In summary, it is my opinion that enough cosmetics have already been developed not to justify hurting animals any further, especially since this is only so that we can look nice. In terms of testing for medicine to help humans, I can accept testing to a certain extent; however, I believe that is probably no longer needed due to our advanced knowledge. I truly hope that the time for animal testing is at an end.

GT 1A

3 Writing a letter of request

Dear Sir/Madam,

I'm writing this letter to enquire about your school and the courses you offer. I'm considering the possibility of travelling to your country to take an English course, but before I do this, I would like some more detailed information.

Could you tell me what levels you offer and how you decide which class is suitable for students? I've been studying English for five years at a school in my home country but I am not confident in my speaking and listening. Since I'm interested in a full-time course, I'd also like to know how many hours I need to study per week.

Of course I don't have any family members in your country so I will need some accommodation. Depending on the cost, I would prefer a home-stay family so that I can practise my English as much as possible. I am also a vegan, which means I don't eat meat, fish or any dairy products. Do you think this will cause any problems? Is it possible to find me a home-stay who can cater to my needs?

Finally, could you forward me some brochures for your courses? If possible, could you include some information on what I can do in my spare time because I don't really know your country very well.

I look forward to hearing from you,
Yours sincerely,

GT 1B

3 Writing a letter of complaint

Dear Sir/Madam,

I am writing to express my dissatisfaction with the service I have received from your taxi company both during my ride and in dealing with my subsequent complaint.
Last Wednesday (12th of May), I took one of your taxis to go to an important business meeting in the city. Although the driver said he knew the address I wanted to go to, he took me to the wrong address. This made me late for my appointment. When I complained about his mistake, he became angry and shouted at me. I refused to pay the fare and he then started to threaten me. I took down his information and left the taxi while he was shouting, and I immediately wrote a letter of complaint to your company. However, I am very disappointed to find that I haven't a letter of apology for the driver's behaviour. As a representative of your company, he should behave in a courteous manner; particularly because it was the driver who had made the mistake.

I would like to recommend that you train your staff to behave in a polite manner to customers. I also expect an apology for your employee's behaviour towards me.

Yours sincerely,
Brian Tan

GT 2

5 Writing a General Training essay

In certain cultures, such as many Asian or Middle Eastern ones, it is common to live in extended families. In these families, weaker or more vulnerable people are protected and taken care of. This sense of responsibility towards other family members is not always shared in all contemporary societies. Yet I believe we have an obligation to try to look after this section of the community.

In my opinion, our society has to provide ways of ensuring that the people who really need help receive it. We cannot always rely on families to give this support, for a variety of reasons. For example, some people don't have time or enough money to look after other family members. In cases such as this, somebody has to help. This is why we need national organisations such as the Salvation Army to look after the vulnerable members of society. These types of groups are private; therefore, they need proper funding. Individuals such as you or I can give donations to help them. What's more, some organisations accept help in other forms: donations of food, clothing or blankets. It is even possible to volunteer your time, by helping at the weekend or in the evening.

Furthermore, the government should use part of the income it receives from our taxes to build and run centres which can cater for the old or the handicapped. Our taxes should be used to benefit our society in this way, in addition to helping the country run efficiently for things like the police and ambulances. By doing this, the government can adopt a nationwide approach and employ suitably qualified staff.

In summary, I strongly believe that it is essential that we take care of the weaker members of society through governmental and private organisations such as the Salvation Army.

5 Academic Writing Task 1: Describing a process

Adult and immature turtles spend most of their time in shallow areas off the coast in order to feed; however, nesting occurs on beaches. Adult turtles migrate to shallow waters when they are ready to breed. This occurs when the turtle is between two and eight years old. The female turtle mates, then swims to a nearby beach to lay her eggs, where they incubate for about 8-10 weeks. This process can be repeated over a period of around two weeks. When the female has finished laying eggs, both she and the males return to foraging areas off the coast.

After the incubation period, the baby turtles, which are called hatchlings, slowly emerge from the sand. Immediately, they move towards the ocean and begin a long period of open ocean foraging. Scientists know very little about the first 20 years of a turtle's life; however, it is believed that the turtles may migrate widely in this time. Turtles can live for many years. It is common for the creature to live for up to fifty years.

1 Studying Overseas

1.1

1   I know lots of people hate travelling by plane, but I enjoy it. I don't mind living out of bags for a short time, so staying in a hotel is not a problem for me. I love the whole experience of a new culture and enjoy meeting new people. What I really hate is coming home again!

2   I can't stand travelling abroad. I don't like foreign food for one thing – it upsets my stomach – and I miss the comforts of home. I'm not keen on plane journeys – I hate being in a tiny space for hours and hours. I'm fond of travel programmes on TV, though, and would rather enjoy foreign countries from my armchair!

1.2

I come from London in the south-east of England. It's a very large city and has a population of about twelve million people. Most people travel into the city every day to work, usually by bus or underground train, which we call the 'tube'. Many people work in offices or for big companies, but of course people do all sorts of jobs here. I think the majority of people live in what we call semi-detached houses, in the suburbs usually, but nearer the centre of the city people live in flats, too. London is great fun because there is so much to do – erm, great restaurants, theatre, museums – but it is very busy so it can be quite stressful as well sometimes. One of the best things about living in London is that it's so cosmopolitan – you know, there's a great mix of people from different countries and cultures. I really love it here and I can't imagine living anywhere else really.

1.3

1   I'm planning to go abroad and have a holiday – I'm so tired of studying! I need a break.

2   I'm probably going to continue my studies in Canada and then become a doctor back in my own country. I've always wanted to be a doctor.

3   I'll get my IELTS results back in September. I'm hoping to study at Exeter University.

4   I don't know if I'll be able to, but I'd really love to study Law in the United States.

5   I need to study English for a few more months, but then I'm definitely going to move to New Zealand straight away.

1.4

1   Where are you planning to study after you take your IELTS exam?

2   What subject do you intend to study?

3   What are your plans for next year?

4   Are you planning any holidays in the near future?

5   What are your long-term plans?

2 Shopping and the Internet

2.1

1   dollar
2   euro
3   pound
4   cent
5   pence or pee

2.2

1   sixty-five dollars
2   eight hundred and fifty pounds
3   one thousand four hundred euros, or fourteen hundred euros
4   ten thousand dollars
5   one million pounds, or a million pounds
6   six dollars fifty
7   ten pounds ninety-nine
8   ninety centss
9   twenty-five pence, or twenty-five pee
10 fifteen euros

2.3

1   These shoes cost me a fortune. They were $350, but I absolutely love them.

2   Have you heard? John's grandmother left him £50,000 in her will ... plus the house!

3
A: Did you manage to sell your car?
B: Yes, but we got €3,000 less than we wanted for it €15,000 in the end.

4
A: How much do I owe you?
B: £2 for the coffee and 3.50 for the sandwich ... so let's see ... that's 5.50 altogether.

5   Mum, I need 80p for the bus. And some money for a drink ...

2.4

A: Have you seen this gadget? It looks amazing.
B: Wow! What is it?
A: It's called a sea scooter.
B: Sea scooter? Scooter ... like a motorbike?
A: Not exactly. This is to help you move more quickly in the water. It can be used underwater at the pool or in the sea.
B: Wow! That's really great! How fast can it go?
A: Oh, only about four kilometres per hour ... but it would be really fun to ride!

B: Expensive?

A: Very. About £300!

B: Where can you buy one?

A: Well, specialist shops and also from the Internet.

2.5

(S = Salesperson; C = Customer)

S: Good morning, what can I do for you?

C: Hi, I'm interested in getting an Internet connection at home and I was wondering what kind of packages you offer.

S: Certainly, Sir. Well, basically, we have two popular schemes for people to choose from: The Heavy Surfer and the Light Surfer packages.

C: I see. Could you tell me a little more about each of them? I mean, what's the difference between them?

S: It all depends on how much you intend to use the Internet. For instance, are you a light user or do you use the Internet often?

C: Hmm. Perhaps you need to tell me about each of the packages in more detail. What are the features of the Heavy Surfer scheme?

S: This one is designed for people who use the Net a lot. It costs $35 a month – which isn't very much, really. This package is very useful if you want to download songs, movies or games. But there's a limit of 500 megabytes.

C: Listening to songs from the Internet? Wow! And it's possible to download movies as well?

S: Yeah, if you are interested in that, you should definitely consider this option.

C: So if I'm interested in downloading movies or playing games, I'd better choose the Heavy Surfer package. OK. What other costs are there?

S: Well, it costs $200 to install, but that covers us coming to your house to install the cable connection, and set up your cable modem for you.

C: Cable means the connection is much faster, doesn't it? Hmm, the problem is, because I'm new to this, I don't know how much I'm going to need. Have you got anything smaller?

S: Yes, of course. Maybe you should consider the Light Surfer package. That's designed for people who don't use the Internet as much. It costs $25 per month – that's enough for emailing your friends and light usage.

C: $25 a month. But I probably want to do more than emailing.

S: Don't worry – you get 200 megabytes of downloads with that.

C: OK, that sounds interesting. Do I need to get cable installed for this?

S: No, this installation is free because you use your existing phone line. The Light Surfer is a dial-up connection, which only uses a telephone modem.

C: I see. Well, thanks for your help. I'll have a think about it.

2.6

A: Here's another amazing gadget to use in the sea.

B: What is it this time?

A: It's called an underwater breather.

B: Who would use one of those? James Bond?

A: Well, probably scuba divers – they would appreciate this.

B: What's so good about it?

A: Well, look at the size – it's the smallest tank of compressed air on the market and really light as well.

B: How big is it then? You can't tell from the picture.

A: About 20cm – not much bigger than a can of drink. Incredible, isn't it?

B: Yeah, if it lasts long enough.

A: Well, it says two minutes or forty breaths.

B: Eat your heart out, James Bond – here comes Stuart Malcolm!

2.7

(S = Salesperson; C = Customer)

S: Good afternoon.

C: Good afternoon. Er, I'm interested in getting an Internet connection.

S: OK, broadband or dial-up?

C: Umm. I don't think we have broadband in my area yet, so dial-up, I think.

S: OK, well, I just need to take down some details from you. What's your full name?

C: Gerrard, John Gerrard.

S: Could you just spell your surname for me?

C: G-E-R-R-A-R-D, like the football player.

S: Yes, I see. And where do you live?

C: In Sherwood, on Winchester Road. Number 129.

S: And is that a house or a flat?

C: It's a house. And the postcode is QLD 4010.

S: OK, right. Oh, and I'm going to need your telephone number, too. The code for Sherwood is 03, isn't it?

C: That's right. It's 03 924 3116.

S: ... 3116. Thanks. Do you have an office number for me as well? Sorry, but we just need it for the form, you see.

C: Oh, that's alright. It's the same code, 03, and the number is 816 4572.

S: OK. How soon do you want to be connected?

C: Well, as soon as possible, really. What's the quickest you can do it?

S: I'm afraid that you've missed the start date this month ... so the next start date is ...

C: July, then. Yes, oh well, I suppose that'll be alright.

S: Yes, July 1st. Sorry about that. Have you decided which scheme you want to have?

C: Do you mean the type of package? Yes, I'm going to go with the Weekend Special – the others don't really suit me.

S: The Weekend Special? Yes, that's one of our most popular packages, actually. I've got that at home myself. Did you know that you get a free gift with that one?

C: Really? That's nice. What is it?

S: Well, there's a choice of a free mousepad or an Austranet pen or cup.

C: Hmm. That's not much of a choice, is it? I'll take the pen – I've already got a mousepad.

S: Right. There you are – your free Austranet pen. Now, how would you like to pay? You can pay by credit card, direct debit or by cheque. Which do you prefer?

C: I haven't actually got a cheque book, so I'll have to pay by credit card.

S: That's fine. OK, I've just got one last question for you. This is for our marketing department. How did you hear about Austranet?

C: Oh, that's easy – a friend of mine told me that you were one of the best service providers. He's been with Austranet for two years.

3 Jobs and Job-hunting

3.1

Ok, well, I once had an interview for a job as an assistant teacher. I was still a student and I was studying Education, but I wasn't qualified at that time so I was only applying to be an assistant. I thought it would be good to get some teaching experience during the long university winter break. Erm, how did I prepare for it? I looked at all my notes again from lectures at university to remind myself of the important things to do with primary school children. I also went to the school's website to get as much information as I could about the place before I went. It was quite a modern primary school with good computer rooms, so I planned to talk about my computer knowledge and how I could use that with the children. What else? Erm, I made a few notes to take into the interview with me in case I got nervous and forgot everything.

So what did they ask me? I can't remember everything they asked – it was quite a long interview – but I remember they asked me about my qualifications and experience with children. They wanted to know why I was applying for the job, of course. One difficult question they asked was about my strengths and weaknesses, which is a tricky one to

answer without saying too many negative things about yourself!

3.2

I'm going to talk about being a musician, which I think would be enjoyable, even though in reality I wouldn't want this job personally.

There are many attractive aspects to this job, I think. First of all, if you are a rock star or pop artist, you'd get to travel a lot, possibly in a private jet if you were really successful. Fans would go crazy about you everywhere you went ... although that could become a disadvantage eventually. On top of that, there would be all the financial advantages: enough money to buy anything you wanted, such as property, cars, clothes or whatever you were interested in ... as well as free gifts or maybe even contracts with companies in return for advertising or endorsing their product. In my opinion, the biggest attraction is of course that you would be doing something you really enjoyed – making music and performing it – which is a dream come true for many amateur musicians.

What about qualifications? Well, I don't think there are any specific requirements as far as qualifications are concerned, but you do need some talent ... or luck ... or both. And finally, what qualities would you need to do this job? Let me think ... I suppose you would need to be an extrovert – it isn't easy to go out on stage in front of thousands of people or to read negative reviews in magazines about your work, for example. Yes, I think the most important thing is not to be too sensitive. And you should be passionate about the music you write or sing as well.

4 Crime and Punishment

4.1

Good evening and thank you for inviting me. I'd like to talk to you tonight about a very serious crime. Now, many of you may not have heard of this particular crime – it is one of the fastest growing crimes in the world and it is called identity theft. You might not even realise that you have been the victim of this crime until much later, long after the event has taken place, but individuals like you can minimise the chance of a successful theft if you know how to protect yourself, which is what I'm going to talk about tonight.

4.2

Identity theft is the unauthorized use of someone's identity to gain a benefit. What that means is a criminal uses your personal information in order to commit a crime – usually financial in nature. A common example of this is using a person's credit card details illegally. It can be devastating to both individuals and businesses. Now, you might be asking yourself 'Why has this type of crime become so common?' Well, the answer is very simple: <u>new technologies,</u> improved telecommunications and the Internet, plus <u>the growth in international trade</u> and financial markets – these have all contributed to the growth of this type of crime. I know it is hard to believe, but yes, the very things that are making our lives easier and more convenient are actually helping certain individuals to commit new types of crime.

4.3

How does a thief get your personal information and what exactly does he steal? I'm sorry to say, that despite your best efforts, there are lots of ways a determined thief can access your personal details. Firstly, there's your wallet or purse. If it is stolen, a thief has access to your <u>driving licence</u>, credit and ATM cards and other personal documents. If you are the victim of a burglary, televisions and stereos may not be the only things that are taken: your personal information and <u>documents</u> might also disappear. I'm sad to say that your mail is also not safe: bank statements, new credit cards, tax returns or <u>cheques</u> – all these items, which carry your personal details, could be of interest to somebody who wants to commit identity theft or fraud. For those of you who use a <u>computer</u>, your personal information is at risk. Computer hackers have the skill to break into your computer while you're using the Internet in order to steal personal information.

4.4

Now I'm sure many of you are feeling a little uncomfortable after hearing that long list of potential risks, and, while it may never be possible to stop identity theft entirely, there are a number of very simple safety measures you can take to protect yourself from becoming a victim of this type of crime. The first step is to <u>improve your security awareness</u>. By this, I mean secure your personal information – don't carry personal details unless you have to; destroy personal documents before throwing them away – why not invest in a small shredding machine, the kind you find in offices everywhere? Check your billing and account records on a regular basis and <u>put security features on your accounts, such as a password</u>. Naturally, you should <u>avoid giving out personal details over the phone</u> or by email as much as possible. And, while we're talking about email, let's turn to the question of computer protection. More and more people use computers and the Internet to communicate, store information and conduct business. It could be your weakest link in avoiding identity theft, so follow these guidelines: always use passwords, and update them regularly; use the latest protection software, including a personal firewall on your computer. This handy piece of software stops people snooping around your computer while you're online. If you want to buy something over the Internet, <u>only use secure</u>

<u>websites</u>. I suggest, too, that you don't use public computers to access personal information.

Finally, in the event of a theft, you should do the following things: report the incident to the police, <u>contact your bank</u>, review your account and credit details very carefully – if necessary, close all accounts and cancel all cards. And don't forget to keep any documentation you have.

Well, that's the end of my talk. I'll take any questions you may have now. Yes, the gentleman in the green shirt ...

4.5

A: So, have you got any ideas for our project?

B: The one where we need to find an example of ways to fight crime? I was thinking about it over the weekend, but I haven't got any ideas yet. What about you?

A: Well, do you remember that <u>documentary</u> I saw a couple of weeks ago that I told you about? The one where modern technology was helping the police?

B: Oh, yes. What exactly was that about? Can you remember?

A: Well, they use police helicopters with <u>video cameras on board to film crimes.</u>

B: Yes, that would be a good one to write about. Hmm. How does it work?

A: Well, helicopters have the advantage of arriving at the crime scene faster than cars on the ground, plus they have a bird's eye view.

B: <u>Right, but how do the police on the ground get the information and catch the criminal?</u>

A: Well, that's the amazing part – the video footage from the camera is sent using satellite technology, so they can see what is happening. It's sent directly to the police vehicles.

B: So you mean they see it exactly as it happens? That's pretty amazing, isn't it?

A: Yes, so criminals are arrested more easily because the police know exactly where to go.

B: And is this a real possibility for the future?

A: <u>It's on trial now</u> in the north-east of England where they have a really high crime rate!

B: Right. That sounds like a good topic for the project, so let's do some research on it. Now, if you find out ...

5 Transport and Inventions

5.1

1 Well, I suppose they partially solve the problem of too many cars on the road. I think any form of public transport is a good idea really, so, yes, <u>I agree up to a point</u> with this statement.

2 Oh, I don't think so. The seat is tiny and you can hardly move for hours at a time. You have to sit next to someone you don't know and ask them to stand up

every time you need to walk about or go to the bathroom. The food is usually awful, as well. <u>No, I don't agree at all.</u>

3 <u>I absolutely agree.</u> If you look at how many roads have been built in the last few decades, it's obvious that the more roads we build, the more cars we produce to fill them up. So building more roads is not the solution in my opinion.

4 That's an interesting possibility. <u>I agree with you to an extent</u>. Making it free may mean more people use it but I don't think it's easy to force people to use public transport because everyone really prefers to use their own car.

5 <u>I don't think so.</u> We can't breathe on the moon, so we'd need very sophisticated equipment to stay there for long periods ... and it will always be dangerous to leave and enter the earth's atmosphere. So, no, I think it's very unlikely.

5.2

1 I think any form of public transport is a good idea really, so, yes, I agree up to a point with this statement.

2 The food is usually awful as well. No, I don't agree at all.

3 I absolutely agree. If you look at how many roads have been built in the last few decades it is obvious that the more roads we build, the more cars we produce to fill them up.

5.3

1 Well, I suppose they partially solve the problem of too many cars on the road. I think any form of public transport is a good idea really, so, yes, <u>I agree up to a point </u>with this statement.

2 Oh, I don't think so. The seat is tiny and you can hardly move for hours at a time. You have to sit next to someone you don't know and ask them to stand up every time you need to walk about or go to the bathroom. The food is usually awful, as well. <u>No, I don't agree at all.</u>

3 <u>I absolutely agree.</u> If you look at how many roads have been built in the last few decades, it's obvious that the more roads we build, the more cars we produce to fill them up. So building more roads is not the solution in my opinion.

4 That's an interesting possibility. <u>I agree with you to an extent</u>. Making it free may mean more people use it but I don't think it's easy to force people to use public transport because everyone really prefers to use their own car.

5 <u>I don't think so.</u> We can't breathe on the moon, so we'd need very sophisticated equipment to stay there for

long periods ... and it will always be dangerous to leave and enter the earth's atmosphere. So, no, I think it's very unlikely.

5.4

1 Will we find an alternative fuel for cars in the near future?

2 Do you think the public transport in your city is adequate?

3 Do you think we should be concerned about pollution caused by cars and other vehicles?

4 Should the government in your country build more roads in your area?

5 Will we be able to go around the world in under twelve hours in the future?

6 Should governments completely ban motorised vehicles?

7 Will we be able to travel to other planets on holidays at some time in the future?

6 The Natural World

6.1

1 Ash and gas clouds often form in the air after volcanic eruptions.

2 The crater is a bowl-shaped opening at the top of the volcano.

3 Lava flow often occurs after a volcanic eruption. Lava is molten rock that comes out from deep within the earth's surface.

4 The main vent is a long, narrow opening in the earth's crust through which hot volcanic materials can escape.

5 A secondary cone is a smaller opening on the side of the volcano, which can emerge following a volcanic eruption.

6 The earth's crust is the outermost, rocky layer of the earth's surface.

7 Deep below the volcano is the magma chamber, which contains vast amounts of molten rock.

6.2

(S = Sam; M = Makoto; C = Chris)

S: Hi, Makoto, Chris. What are you doing?

M: Hello, Sam. Chris and I are just trying to finish the preparations for our tutorial presentations for tomorrow.

C: <u>Yes, that's right</u>. It's really interesting. We're going to be talking about volcanoes.

S: <u>Oh, sounds great</u>. Can you tell me a bit about it now?

M: OK, well, although the general topic is volcanoes, we're going to talk specifically about the 'The Ring of Fire'.

S: The Ring of Fire? <u>Sorry, I don't know what you mean</u>. Sounds like something from a fantasy movie, like *The Lord of the Rings*!

C: Yeah, I agree, it does! I suppose it is kind of magical, actually, but not in the way you're thinking.

S: Uh? I don't follow you.

C: Well, the Ring of Fire refers to a volcanically active region surrounding the Pacific Ocean. This zone of volcanoes passes through several regions: New Zealand, Fiji, Papua New Guinea, the Philippines, up through Japan and into Alaska, then down through the USA and Central and South America.

S: Mm, like a giant circle of fire.

M: Exactly!

S: Wow, that's interesting. There must be a lot of volcanoes there.

M: You're right, there are hundreds, actually, but not all of them are active. And even the ones that are considered active don't necessarily erupt ...

6.3

(S = Sam; M = Makoto; C = Chris)

S: ... So, Makoto, Chris, you have to give your talk on volcanoes today, don't you?

M: Yes, that's right.

C: Yeah, I think we're about ready for it.

S: So, tell me more about what you learned. Did you find out how many volcanoes erupt each year?

M: Yes, Chris did some reading on that.

C: Well, I found out about 50 to 60 volcanoes erupt every year.

S: 50 to 60? Wow, no way! And how many of these eruptions take place in the Ring of Fire?

C: A lot of them, because that whole area is extremely active. For example, the most active volcano in the world is Kilauea in Hawaii. It has eruptions really often, about 20 to 30 times a year, which means it's almost constantly active. Yasur Volcano, in Vanuatu, has had small eruptions 10 to 20 times per hour for the last 800 years!

S: Every hour?! You're kidding!

C: Really, it's true!

S: And so why are there so many volcanoes on the Ring of Fire?

C: Ah, well, that's because most of the world's subduction zones are also located around the Pacific.

S: Subduction? I don't know what that is.

M: Well, you've heard of tectonic plates, haven't you? Most scientists and geologists believe that the surface of the earth – the crust – is broken into about ten large plates which are moving over time. Most geologic activity takes place at the edges of these plates. A subduction zone is where one plate moves under another plate.

S: Oh, I get it. So you mean volcanoes are usually found where those tectonic plates meet?

M: Yes, that's right – and not just volcanoes but also earthquakes and mountain ranges too. The Ring of Fire is where a number of plates meet, which is why so many volcanoes have been formed around the Pacific.

S: Mm, I see ...

6.4

(S = Sam; M = Makoto; C = Chris)

S: ... So, are there different types of volcanoes? They can't be all the same, right?

M: No, that's right. Most vulcanologists ...

S: Sorry? Vulcan ...?

C: Vulcanologists – they're the scientists who study volcanoes.

S: Oh, I see.

M: Well, most of them believe that there are three main types of volcanoes. Most of the volcanoes around the Ring of Fire are what's known as composite volcanoes, but the largest type is called a shield volcano.

S: Shield volcano?

M: Yes. These are very broad, low-lying volcanoes – some of them are over a hundred kilometres wide.

C: They have very gradual slopes, usually between three and ten degrees, so from the side they look like a shield lying on the ground.

M: The most famous example – and the largest – is Mauna Loa in Hawaii, but there are also shield volcanoes in Iceland, the Galapagos Islands ...

S: But you said most of the volcanoes in the Ring of Fire were something else?

M: Right. Most of the ones around the Pacific are what's known as composite volcanoes – these are more like what you'd imagine a volcano to look like, you know, gentle slopes at the bottom then steep slopes rising to a summit, with a small crater at the top.

S: And composite volcanoes can be found all around the Pacific?

C: That's right – in North and South America, Japan, the Philippines. Mt. Fuji is one of the most famous examples.

S: So, there are shield volcanoes, composite volcanoes ... and what's the other type?

M: Cinder cones. These are the smallest kind, usually not more than 300 metres tall, and have straight sides with steep slopes.

C: And they're found where?

C: All over. Some cinder cones form on the slopes of larger shield or composite volcanoes, as secondary cones.

S: So that seems pretty clear – three types: shield volcanoes, composite volcanoes and cinder cones.

M: Actually, there are some other types, like spatter cones, hydrovolcanic vents, and so on ...

S: Well, seems like you certainly know your stuff. Anyway, good luck with the presentation.

M: Yeah, thanks.

C: See you later, Sam.

6.5

(A = Announcer; SM = Sarah MacKenzie)

A: Well, my next guest is Sarah MacKenzie, a zoologist at the Natural History Museum, who's here to talk about their latest conservation project, which is causing a great deal of excitement in this country and overseas. Sarah, could you tell us about what you're doing at the museum?

SM: Sure, thanks, David. Well, our new project, which is supported by the Natural History Museum, the Zoological Society of London and Nottingham University, is called 'The Frozen Ark'. Now many of you will recognise the name 'Ark' from its religious connections: it is the ship that Noah was said to have used to rescue all the animals during the Great Flood. And, indeed, that is sort of the purpose of our project.

A: That sounds like a big task, how are you going to go about it?

SM: Well, we plan to preserve the DNA, or the 'life codes' of thousands of endangered species, so that, in the event that the animals become extinct, future generations of scientists will be able to use the information for study in this field, and, perhaps ultimately this will assist in future conservation initiatives. Experts believe that as many as 10,000 species are currently endangered, and that includes an amazing twenty-five percent of known mammals and a tenth of all recorded bird species which are at risk.

A: Wow, that's a lot of endangered species.

SM: Yes, it really is, so I'm sure you can easily understand the concern of the scientific community, as well as naturalists and ordinary people when it comes to measures to conserve and protect our world's biodiversity. The end of a species leaves a hole in the ecosystem, but it also takes with it a vast amount of biological and genetic information, including all the adaptations that the animal, bird or insect has undergone. To use an analogy from computers rather than biology, what we are attempting to do here is save a back-up copy – the genetic codes of these animals will be stored in a database.

A: I see.

6.6

(A = Announcer; SM = Sarah MacKenzie)

A: So, Sarah, how exactly is the whole thing done?

SM: Well, in practical terms, this will require us to extract tissue samples from animals currently endangered; of course, we don't want to destroy the animal whilst doing so, so the plan is to take a small piece of skin while the animal is sedated. However, with an insect, it will probably mean taking the whole creature. Next, we will transfer the sample to one of our Frozen Ark laboratories and store it at extremely low temperatures. The plan is have a number of such labs all around the world.

A: I see. How long do you think that the DNA samples will last in storage?

SM: Don't worry. We believe that DNA can last tens of thousands of years. And if storage of cells and DNA is successful, we hope that future generations of scientists will not only study them, but even use the DNA to clone. Cloning at the present time is not sophisticated enough to be able to do this, but there is no reason to suppose that it won't be possible in the future. We don't know where the Ark will end up, but it is an important, if not essential step in helping the conservation effort. I'm sure Noah himself would be very proud of this project!

A: I'm sure he would be. Thanks, Sarah, your project sounds fascinating. Now, let's take a few questions from callers …

7 Food and Diet

7.1

Speaker 1

Okay, erm, I'm going to talk about the meal we usually eat at Christmas in my country. We call it Christmas Dinner and it is eaten either on Christmas Eve or on Christmas Day – it depends on the family. It is a really important family occasion so we generally eat it at home or at the home of a close relation such as our grandparents. Some families celebrate with just the close family but some have the extended family there as well, so there can be many people at the table.

I'll explain the details of the meal to you. It takes many hours to prepare and so everyone helps … for example, to prepare vegetables or to lay the table. We decorate the table with Christmas things and maybe some paper hats to wear as well. The main dish usually consists of turkey with stuffing, though I think some families eat other meats such as pork, duck or goose. At my house, Mum is in charge of the turkey because she is so good at it. She roasts the whole turkey in the oven for several hours and the smell is really good. We also have lots of roast vegetables with the turkey, especially potatoes and then we do carrots and broccoli and lots of gravy to go with it. We carry the whole cooked turkey to the dinner table and someone carves it at the table and then we help ourselves to all the other food. It is a very heavy meal so we always feel very full afterward and need a rest before we have dessert. The traditional dessert is Christmas pudding – or plum pudding – which is made with dried fruit several weeks before. Then we can't move for a few hours because we've eaten too much, so we watch TV and chat. I love Christmas dinner – it's my favourite meal of the whole year.

Speaker 2

I'd like to tell you about something special we eat in Germany although it isn't exactly a meal or a dish. We eat these at Easter and they are called 'ostereier' which in English means ... erm ... Easter eggs.

First we boil the eggs until they are hard and then leave them to go cold. Then we colour them with food dye and paint them. If you like, you can buy decorations for the eggs at some shops as well. When they are finished, parents hide them in the garden before the children get up. The children go into the garden with a basket and collect the eggs and then the whole family eat them for breakfast. These days, some families buy chocolate eggs to hide but traditionally we use real eggs. Eggs are important at Easter because they symbolise spring and new life.

Another thing we do with the eggs at Easter is to make an Easter tree and decorate the tree with painted eggs. To do this we make two small holes in a fresh egg and blow out the inside. We rinse the eggs and then paint them with all sorts of colourful designs. We hang these eggs on the 'osterbaum' or Easter tree.

I love Easter eggs as they remind me of happy times with my family when I was young.

7.2

1   Tell me about the diet of people in your country or area.
2   Compare the diet of people in your country today with thirty years ago.
3   Can you explain why diets have changed over the last few decades?
4   How similar or different is food in your country to the countries nearby?
5   Should people be able to kill animals for food?
6   Do people need to be better educated about food and nutrition?
7   People are getting fatter in many countries. Why do you think this is happening?
8   In many places in the world, people are hungry or dying of starvation. Do you think we will ever get rid of this problem?

8   Sickness and Health

8.1

Parts of the body: blood, digestive system, gallbladder, immune system, intestines, kidney, liver, lungs, stomach
Health and sickness: cure, discomfort, illness, injury, pain, recover, symptom, treatment
Food and diet: vitamins, nutrients, minerals

8.2

1   ... So, as you can see, proper care of our livers can assist greatly in our overall sense of well-being. Before we finish today, an interesting fact connected to the liver ...
2   ... and poor sanitation can contribute very heavily to the rate of disease in a city. There are a number of factors which need to be taken into account when discussing ...
3   ... helps to improve our electrolyte and water balance. Let's move on to look at the relationship between the liver and the gallbladder. If you ...
4   ... one of the best ways is to increase your heart rate. For instance, exercising regularly can dramatically improve ...
5   ... occasionally leading to severe liver damage. As a result of this the patient may need a liver transplant.
6   Exercising is certainly a good way to burn calories. Not only that, it can help you keep the weight off, even when ...
7   ... have shown for many years how detrimental it is to health. On the other hand, the huge amounts of money the government receives in duty from its sale ensures that ...
8   Despite years of research into liver function and the causes of liver diseases, the average person still has a very poor understanding of how it works. Personally, I think that our system of education should focus more ...

8.3

Good morning and welcome to the last in the series in the Bridging Course to Medical Science. This morning we look at the liver and health issues related to it.

What is the liver and what does it do? Well, the liver is the largest organ in the abdomen, weighing from one to two point five kilograms. We can describe the liver as the body's main filter; it receives most of the nutrients (as well as the toxins) absorbed from the bowel and co-ordinates their use. It then removes much of what the body doesn't need or whatever is potentially dangerous to the body if it accumulates in large quantities. This could happen, for example, by consuming alcohol and even as a result of taking too many medicines.

Although the main function is filtering blood and removing harmful substances, there are several other roles. It stores <u>extra blood</u> for emergencies, and creates substances that enhance our immune system (such as gamma globulin). Not only that: the liver also stores vitamins, minerals and sugars and helps the body access the <u>energy</u> we need from proteins, fats and carbohydrates.

8.4

Let's move on to look at the relationship between the liver and the gallbladder; an extremely important one, because many health problems can be traced back to problems with the liver. On the diagram here, we can see the <u>liver</u> on the far left and on the opposite side is the <u>stomach</u>. We also have the pancreas shown there as well so you get an idea of the proportions. Now the small bag-like elastic structure, tucked underneath the liver, is the gallbladder. So how does this relationship work? Well, bile, the substance that helps <u>break down food</u>, is produced in the liver and stored in the gallbladder. From there, it is then excreted, or 'released', to break down fats and to do this it goes down the bile duct into the duodenum at this point here. If the bile becomes too thick, or stagnates, gallstones can develop. These tiny stones can sometimes <u>cause blockages</u> in the bile duct, causing great discomfort to the sufferers and although we can get rid of them, it is generally a painful process. The duodenum is in fact the beginning of the <u>small intestine</u>, which leads in turn to the large intestine.

8.5

In ancient societies, the healers of the past understood that when our bile is stagnant and does not flow smoothly, problems with the liver result. <u>Chinese medicine relates anger with poor liver and gallbladder function. The Greeks believed that sadness was also the result of liver problems:</u> did you know, for example, the word 'melancholy' comes from the Greek 'melanos' (black) and 'chole' (bile) – or, 'black bile'?

Apart from gallstones, poor care of our livers can also lead to <u>poor skin tone</u>, acne, problems with blood clotting, poor vision and even immune system breakdown, as the liver is holding onto toxic substances which would normally be cycled out of the body in the bile. So, as you can see, proper care of our livers can assist greatly in our overall sense of well-being.

Before we finish today, an interesting fact connected to the liver. Did you know that in some cultures, the liver is considered so important to health that when people get married, <u>the groom promises his liver to the bride</u>, not his heart?

<u>In today's drugs-and-surgery approach to healthcare, the understanding of how to take proper care of the liver is often ignored,</u> but I hope I have managed to impress on you the importance of this vital organ and the role it plays.